urban**tapestry**

editorial committee

Sandy Eisenberg Sasso, Editor

Nancy Niblack Baxter

S. L. Berry

Dan Carpenter

Judith Vale Newton

Barbara Shoup

photography

Kim Charles Ferrill

project coordinator

Tess Baker

INDIANA
University Press
Bloomington & Indianapolis

urban tapestry *indianapolis stories*

This book is a publication of

Indiana University Press
601 North Morton Street
Bloomington, Indiana 47404-3797 USA

http://iupress.indiana.edu

Telephone orders   800-842-6796
Fax orders   812-855-7931
Orders by email   iuporder@indiana.edu

The paper used in this publication meets the minimum
requirements of American National Standard for Information
Sciences—Permanence of Paper for Printed Library
Materials, ANSI Z39.48-1984.

Manufactured in the United States of America

Library of Congress Cataloging-in-Publication Data

Urban tapestry : Indianapolis stories / editorial committee,
Sandy Eisenberg Sasso, editor ... [et al.] ; photography Kim
Charles Ferrill; project coordinator Tess Baker.
      p. cm.
 ISBN 0-253-21544-7 (pbk. : alk. paper)
 1. Indianapolis (Ind.)—Social conditions. I. Title: India-
napolis stories. II. Sasso, Sandy Eisenberg. III. Ferrill, Kim
Charles. IV. Baker, Tess.
 HN80.I54 U7 2002

                              2002002911

1 2 3 4 5 07 06 05 04 03 02

The Beginning of the Story

A city rich in its blessings of red ripened tomatoes and yellow sweet corn is often viewed as monochromatic in its human bounty. But on a hot day in July, life in the city tells a different story. My husband, who is from Panama, and I meet a Sikh friend and his family for lunch in an Indian restaurant in a trendy part of the city. As we enter, we are welcomed by a Muslim physician, who is a spokesperson for Islam in the community and a good friend. Seated next to our table are two ministers, one a professor at Christian Theological Seminary and the other a leading Methodist pastor. Halfway through our meal, a member of my synagogue joins the luncheon crowd. Here we are, Jew, Muslim, Sikh, and Christian sipping sweet Indian tea prepared with milk and spiced with cardamom. Hebrew, Punjabi, and English mix freely with curried rice and Tandoori cooking. This is not the Indianapolis most people expect to find. The stories in this collection bear testimony to a reality beyond the stereotypes.

In fact, the life of a city depends on the stories it chooses to tell and to hear. Usually, those who get to tell their stories are individuals who do something extraordinarily good or bad. But the blood of the city flows with the stories of the everyday, the triumphs and failures, the accomplishments and defeats that make up the landscape of urban life.

The Urban Tapestry Project was designed to take the pulse of the city through the stories of its people. Although the focus is Indianapolis, the issues this book addresses apply to all urban centers. They may be grounded in the unique geography and personality of the Hoosier capital, but they transcend their particular locale to speak to the universal human condition.

When the project began, I wondered how it would be possible to get people to talk about events in their lives that were both intimate and often deeply disturbing. To my surprise, I and the other writers discovered that it was not necessary to devise a way to get people to talk; we simply needed to allow them the opportunity to speak. Too often, people do not have anyone to whom to tell their story. And when we bury our stories out of fear that others will reject them or ignore them, we lose a piece of ourselves. To the people who graciously opened for us a small window into their lives, we can offer the gift of someone who listens.

We can discover the history of Indianapolis through encyclopedic articles on major events, social change, and economic and demographic trends. We can view Hoosier mythology in the slogans that have come to identify this place—The Crossroads of America, The Amateur Sports Capital, A Slice of the Heartland. We can analyze the city through the eyes of the social scientist, the politician, the urban planner; or we can capture the soul of the city through the stories of its people.

This collection invites readers to better understand urban life by hearing from the people who make their homes in the city. The vignettes collected by writers, journalists, and folklorists create a narrative album that expresses the view from the business office to the front porch, from the conference table to the kitchen table, from the Speedway to the high school track. They talk about race, education, crime, alienation, and community. They give us a glimpse into how we celebrate and how we grieve. They include the voices of a diverse population of different ages from a variety of neighborhoods and ethnic backgrounds.

The stories do not make a uniform cloth. One strand is woven together with another to create a tapestry. It reminds us that more than one thing can be true at the same time, that contrary and contrasting experiences make up the warp and woof of the fabric of society. Acts of forgiveness are intertwined with unresolved pain, hospitality with rejection, compassion with cruelty.

Dividing the four sections of the collection and interspersed throughout the stories are quotes from the sacred writings of the many faith traditions that make up our urban communities. These sources are meant to serve as standards against which we may judge the quality of urban life.

These narratives are not all there is to say about life in Indianapolis. Many more stories wait to be told and heard, among them are our neighbor's story and our own. This collection is meant to foster a conversation about who we are and what we want to become.

Sandy Eisenberg Sasso

A Second Look

Pictures tell their own stories. The eye of the camera seeks to capture the high speed of the city living in a frozen frame. The camera takes in images in wide full strokes and small slashes, like a painter wielding an array of brushes.

A slow shutter speed blurs the figures of two businessmen as they pass. They appear to move quickly and purposefully in contrast to the homeless people wandering aimlessly in the background. I focus the lens across the face of a blind man who sells brooms for a living and make images he will never see.

I throw a line of focus across the face on the Christ statue at St. Mary's Church and let everything else go out of focus. An altar boy from a nearby Hispanic congregation quietly takes his place in front of Jesus. They are friends, and together they form the image the camera captures. The blurred background becomes a space for others to find their own place.

In my frame, the old downtown buildings and mansions on Meridian Street are more than architectural structures. They house the narratives of peoples' lives—how they work and make love, argue and make peace, grieve and make good.

I look for sights not so much seen as felt. Only when I am held by the moment can I hold the vision still and let it appear to be in motion. Some images are there for the seeing; others are hidden, often fading into anonymity.

The photographs in this collection are a city's portraits. They invite us to take a second look at our urban tapestry and perhaps to form a new vision of what is and what might be.

Kim Charles Ferrill

acknowledgments

Urban Tapestry was born out of a desire to create a vehicle for public teaching, to communicate the triumphs and failures of city life to all its citizens. It began with the vision of David Bodenhamer and The Polis Center of IUPUI who understood the power of narrative to capture the imagination and to provide a catalyst for conversation and change.

This collection of stories was made possible through generous funding from the Lilly Endowment, Inc., and the continued support of Polis and its staff. A special thank you goes to Tess Baker, whose administrative support was tireless and exacting.

The members of the editorial committee spent endless hours collecting and editing the many stories of this volume. Their keen eye for detail, their creative talents, and their knowledge of the diverse landscape of this city have finely woven the threads of this urban tapestry.

Janet Allen, director of the Indianapolis Repertory Theater, provided invaluable advice throughout the project. Hande Birkalan spent months interviewing people throughout the city and contributed greatly to this collection.

Most of all, this gathering of voices exists because of the many people who were willing to share their stories. Even in a city as well designed as Indianapolis, it is possible to lose one's way. The stories in these pages provide a map for our city's soul.

urban tapestry

justice and kindness and giving to kinsfolk

For our early Biblical ancestors, the sacred found its home in the simple life of the desert, not in the city. It accompanied the shepherd; it dwelled in tents. But the prophet Isaiah also reminds us that the whole earth is full of God's glory. So where does the sacred exist in modern cities? Today, we most probably would look to the cathedrals, churches, synagogues, and mosques that transfigure the urban skyline, those traditional places of religious gathering, as our holy markers.

Yet, to explore the holy in the midst of city life is to seek out its people, not simply those whom we recognize on our daily commutes, in our offices, in the shopping malls, and on our neighborhood streets, but also individuals who are often hidden from our view, the people on the margins. Our city jaunts typically do not take us to soup kitchens, isolated street corners, alley ways, and prisons. Despite a jogging path that cuts through the heart of the city, we rarely cross paths with a forty-year-old who is learning to read for the first time, a woman thrown out of her apartment with her children, a convict doing community clean-up. Yet the image of God resides in these urban dwellers as well.

We measure city life by many standards: economic stability, employment rate, safety, cultural offerings. Among those standards are the ones that tell us how to treat the individuals who, at first glance, are easy to overlook. The stories in the next few pages invite you to listen to urban dwellers who frequently do not have a voice.

Lo! God has enjoined upon you justice and kindness and giving to kinsfolk.

—Quran 16:19

I'm the Loneliest Person in the World

It was Christmas Eve, December 1975, the year before I was ordained as an Episcopal priest. I had no church to go to. In those days, there were no places for us as female religious leaders. I remember leaving my house. Everyone was having a good time, and no one wanted to go with me. I went downtown alone and decided to go to Christ Church Cathedral. I started around the Circle. It was a very snowy night. Suddenly, I heard a noise. This inebriated soul came walking out from between two buildings. At first, I was scared. But he said, "Would you just talk to me?"

And I said, "Sure."

Then he asked, "What are you doing out here?"

I had my coat open at the top and he could see my collar. I said, "I'm getting ready to go into the Cathedral for church. What are you doing out here?"

He said, "I don't have a church. I don't have anybody. Will you talk to me?"

And we talked. We talked about how he hated God, how he thought the whole issue of Christmas was ridiculous. He had never felt the sense of God in any way, shape, or form. He felt abandoned. His family had abandoned him. He felt that God had done it. His only experience of God was that of abandonment, " . . . if that was God," he said.

Then he asked me, "Why are you so tied into something that you cannot touch or see?" I told him, "Well, I am not sure. I don't really have that answer. Yet something inside of me says that I don't want to be alone. And if I don't want to be alone, I need to know what faith is about. I need to know that there is a power greater than I am that keeps me from being alone, that I can turn to no matter what."

He said, "I don't have that."

And I asked, "Why, not?"

He said, "You have to go to church for that."

"No," I responded, "you don't have to go to church. We have it right now. You are talking to me, aren't you? And I'm talking to you. We're expressing our needs to each other. For me, that's where God is right here."

We kept walking a little farther. I asked if he had eaten anything, and he said he had not. There was a Subway shop around the corner, and we went in. It was about 10:30 p.m., and I got something for him to eat and coffee for both of us. He just kept staring at me. I said, "Is there something you want to say?"

He replied, "Yea, I'm the loneliest person in the world."

Then I began to tell him some of my story, about how going into the church ended my marriage, about the fact that none of my children wanted anything to do with religion. So I told him, "I lost a lot, too. You aren't the only one who has lost a lot."

He looked at me and said, "I'm just amazed that we are talking."

We went on talking until it was time to go to Mass. I told him, "I would love to have you come with me."

He refused, "Oh no, I won't come with you."

But as we neared the Cathedral, I threw my arms around him and he threw his arms around me. I'll never forget that.

I said, "I want to thank you for making a very special night of my life not so lonely." And he said the same thing.

He went on down the street, and I went into the church.

Interview by Sandy Eisenberg Sasso

The Reverend Natalia Beck is an author, speaker, and spiritual facilitator. She was the second woman ordained as an Episcopal priest in the United States and the first to organize a battered woman's shelter. She was founder and Executive Director of the Julian Center and Director of Human Relations for the City of Indianapolis. She is the founder of The Pilgrimage Institute for Integrative Healing in Largo, Florida, and is a Holbrook Fellow at Mind | Body | Medical Institute, Harvard Medical School.

My Kids Hated It Bad

They asked me to leave. My kids hated it bad. It was four days before Christmas . . . and I had all my Christmas stuff there. When the police came, they had movers with them, and they took my kids' Christmas. They took it. It was all wrapped up underneath the tree. They even took my Christmas tree. They took everything . . . from my beds to my entertainment center, to my kitchen things, pots and pans, glasses, everything. They moved all my things out and put it in storage, and they're chargin' me $400 to get it out.

That day was a bad day. I couldn't do nothing but cry. That apartment was everything to me. I will never forget it until the day I die. They didn't have to do me like that. But I think God just wanted a change for me and wanted my kids out of there.

My kids, they keep askin' me, "You still got our presents?" And I said, "the apartment people took them." I couldn't do nothin' but tell them the truth. I told them they put me out because of that incident with Shareena. I had to tell them the truth about that. And, really, they've been understandin'. They keep sayin', "We'll be all right. When are you goin' get us another place?"

I'm workin' on it every day. That's all they look forward to. I have a son that's eight years old, and a daughter that's seven. And I'm currently takin' care of my sister's kids. They're twins. They are eight . . . be nine in June, and I sometimes take care of their little sister. She's two. The reason I'm keepin' my sister's kids is that she's incarcerated. I've had her kids ever since they was six months . . . and now they're eight.

After we had to leave our place, I took the kids over to my auntie's house because she had a whole house, and she had an apartment upstairs. But it needed a new furnace, so I didn't want to stay there. It was too much money, and I didn't have the money to put in a furnace. The neighborhood was bad too, so I didn't want to stay there.

So I went to my grandmother's house to stay. I was there, and she didn't want me to put my kids in school there. She was talkin' about how it might mess with her Social Security, or her rent man wouldn't want the kids there. So I had a friend that works at this shelter, and she told me that this would be the best place for me and my kids. She said they'd help us.

It was hard to come here. I was basing what I thought about homeless shelters on "he says, she says" because I had never been in a shelter before. The lady that referred me to it said, "It's not that bad. All you have to do is come and see how it is."

Actually, Dayspring is better than my grandmother's house. The people are nice, and they're here to help you. It's kinda comfortable. I gotta look at the bright side of it. I could be sleepin' on the streets with the kids. Or goin' to people that really don't want you in their home. They might let you in for a few days, but these people at the shelter let you stay until you're able to move out.

So we're here. I put my kids in school here, and I get up every morning, trying to find a job in the city. I want to work in a hospital. I put in a few applications at the hospitals, at Wishard and University Hospital. That's mainly where I'm goin', somewhere in a hospital. They can start me in environmental, you know . . . housekeepin', laundry. I can start there and move my way up. Oh, and I put an application in for the kitchen there, too.

When I get out of here, I'm goin' forward. I'm not goin' backwards. I want a house . . . I would love to own my own house. All I have to do is start in the right direction. Get a good-paying job. I'd rather work than be on welfare. I don't know . . . I guess God has just blessed me. He's not makin' me just worry. That's past tense. You know, it's behind me. I can't dwell on it anymore. I gotta stay strong for my kids. I want to keep my little family together.

Interview by Judith Vale Newton

❋

This single twenty-nine-year-old woman and her children were evicted from a public housing project in Indianapolis. At the time of this interview, she and the children were living at Dayspring Center, a shelter for homeless families in downtown Indianapolis.

The Alley

The men arrived in a large white bus and slowly emerged to make their way to the coffee. There was little talk as they drank. One man had a look on his face that said he had not been up this early on a Saturday morning in a long time. He sucked his coffee as if he needed it badly. His clothes did not match and had not seen an iron in quite a while; his shoes were old loafers speckled with white paint. His hair was standing straight up, as if he'd just pulled a sweater over his head. Most of the men had a similar dazed look. It was cold outside, and each stood, staring blankly, with one ungloved hand shoved in a pocket, and one holding the warm cup of coffee near his face.

My assignment was to photograph these men who had been convicted of crimes and were now doing community service for the remainder of their sentences. A neighborhood group supervised them as they cleaned alleys in an old west-side neighborhood. Loading my cameras, I worried a little about the cooperation of the men and the images I would get of them.

"Get the rakes over here and bring me some trash bags," the supervisor said. A young woman who worked with him left to do as he said. Her son was playing with a plastic replica of a "butterfly" knife. When he showed it to the youngest of the men in the group, the man took it and gave it a flick of his wrist. The plastic blade emerged from the handle and snapped into place. The boy watched, fascinated, as the man flicked it open and closed several times. He reached for the toy to try it himself just as the supervisor appeared. "Give me that thing!" he said. The supervisor snatched the knife from the young man and hurled it into the backyard of the house where we had gathered, startling the group to attention. He handed out the rakes and trash bags. "Goddamn it, let's get to work. You can pick up all the crap in the alley, but don't set foot in anyone's yard."

The men set to work, and the woman and her son helped. The little boy ran back and forth from his mother to the men, and I photographed him working. I explained to the men what I was doing and asked if it was all right to photograph them, too. A tough-looking black man placed his face six inches from mine and said, "You take my picture, and I'll sue your ass." I looked him straight in the eye and replied, "Won't get nothin'." A long two seconds passed and a broad smile broke the surface of his cold dark face. "This guy is all right," he said. Minutes later, when I took a close-up of him working, he smiled again.

Halfway through the morning's work, the three neighborhood supervisors left to oversee some municipal workers who had arrived to remove a large bush from the side of the street. "How does it feel to be alone in an alley with twelve convicted criminals?" one of the men asked. I smiled, turned my back on him, and concentrated on the image in my lens—all the while listening carefully behind me.

The men talked to me off and on. "This is a good job," one said. "We get four hours of community service for only an hour-and-a-half of work." The young man who had shown his skill with the knife said, "No shit? Will I only have to do half the time of my community service?" "No," somebody else said. "It's just, if you're smart, you'll figure out which ones are the least amount of work. They ain't all like this job. But you gotta do a good job, or somebody will give you a bad report, and then they can stick you with whatever they want. And don't not show up when you're supposed to. They don't like that."

I held a trash bag open while one of the men placed a stinking heap of garbage in it. He spilled some, then bent and scooped it up and placed it in the bag. "Thanks, man," he said. He took the bag from me, expertly tied it into a knot. I photographed him carrying the bag to the side of the alley, then focused on the words "crack house" painted on the fence against which the bags were placed. "That's only one of many, my man," he said.

When their work was finished, the men gathered back by the coffee. The box of two dozen donuts that had been set out remained virtually untouched, and a homeless woman stood looking at them. "Take some," I said. "Take eight." She quickly did so and was gone.

The supervisor appeared, complaining about the quality of the work. "See what I told you?" he said to me. "It's always this way." I turned my back without a word and made a photograph of the bus pulling up to take the men away. The men threw their coffee cups in a trash bag, and several of them shook my hand and said, "Thanks." The boy waved good-bye to them, and they waved back. His mother gathered the rakes and placed them in a pile.

Walking back to my car, I looked down one of the alleys where the men had worked. The tallest of the downtown buildings was framed at the end of it. Beneath the buildings, thousands of pieces of clear and green glass sparkled in the morning sun. I made that photograph and put my camera on the seat beside me.

When the busload of men passed me, I waved, wondering if our paths would ever cross again. I picked up my camera and made the last image of the day.

Kim Charles Ferrill

That Wasn't My Way of Cooking

I made up my mind that this was a mission sent to me from God. It all got started because I was taking care of the kids in my neighborhood who were fighting. I was a lonely widow and the mother of ten children who were all grown when I started refereeing the fights of these kids. They were trampling my grass on their way to a school on the street behind my house. I began a Bible class in the yard of my home for them, serving some goodies to get their attention. When you live in a neighborhood of poverty-stricken, one-parent families, food will get the attention of any child.

Things were going well with these kids when I heard that the All Saints Church kitchen was going to open for the poor, for anyone who wanted to eat, so I brought them here to eat. In coming here, I saw that people of all cultures were coming to get a free meal . . . and they were in desperate need of help. There were old men and old women whose footsteps were very slow, coming in for lunch. Some folk even had been eating from garbage cans . . . eating whatever way they could. Garbage cans in Indianapolis!

I had always considered myself a poor person until then. And when I saw the needs of all of these other people, I felt really blessed. When I was asked by a lady to volunteer, I did right away. I worked in the kitchen, preparing the food. When this lady who initially opened the place would want to go shopping or something, she would say to me, "Hey, how about cooking for me today?" And I would tell her, "Oh, I don't know how to do this. I don't know how to cook for this many people." She would answer me, "This pan holds 48 cups. And every time you see another person come in, you know, put in another cup."

But that wasn't my way of cooking. My way of cooking was preparing what I would want to eat. I looked at it as cooking for my family, so the government's meat and noodles—half-cooked with no seasonings—had to go. I went out and bought some shoulder bones and fatback and onions and cooked a pot of beans. I served them, along with some southern cornbread, milk, juice, coffee, and some fruit. It worked! Many times, when the weather got real bad, a doctor's wife who was on the church board and I would take jars of soup and some crackers and doughnuts, and go out to search for these people. When we would find them, it was very heart-touching. Most of the time, they would be in some one-room apartment downtown, and there would be maybe four other guys there. They'd all have their little corners and their little bottles of wine and their overcoat or maybe a blanket, if they were lucky.

We would walk in, and I'd say to them, "Hey, I want to give you this food I have in exchange for the bottle you have." They would give me their wine bottles, and I would give them some hot soup and crackers and doughnuts. It was a search of joy for us. You know, the joy that you would see in their eyes for having a warm meal. It was enough to make you want to come back again.

After six months, the lady running the kitchen decided she didn't want anything to do with it anymore. She asked me, "Do you want this position? It's not going to last. The soup kitchen's not going to last." She quit because she thought when the government food was gone, that would be it. But I saw all that need. I began to pray about it and asked God for direction as to what to do and how to do it, because I knew these people needed help . . . and so I ended up taking things over at the food program.

Regardless of how raggedy or dirty or how hard these people look, underneath those clothes there's a soul in them that needs to be touched by somebody. I know that love will change things. If you love your neighbor as yourself, you'll do something about it. And that is a part of my Christian belief, to help people help themselves.

Interview by Judith Vale Newton

꙳

Nellie M. Gold is the Food Director for Dayspring Center, a shelter for homeless families in downtown Indianapolis. The mother of ten children, the grandmother of twenty, and the great-grandmother of twenty more, "Miss Nellie" has served the homeless since 1983. What began as a soup kitchen to feed twenty-five or thirty people has become a large-scale food ministry that provides as many as 120,000 meals a year under her guidance.

I Had to Back Up and Listen

Back then, there was lots of child abuse. Back then, they called it "chastising." But it wasn't . . . it was abuse. I remember, when I went to stay with my dad in Georgia for a while, how my stepmother would fill the stove up in her bedroom with wood and coal, and the whole belly of the stove would get hot. It got red. Then she made me sit behind it. My face blistered, and when my dad asked her what happened, she told him that I was playin' too close to the stove. She didn't tell him that she made me sit behind the stove. It was so hot, and I was so close. I was up against the wall until you couldn't go back any further, trying to get away from it. I was really tiny. If I had leaned forward, I would have burnt.

I got sent to live with Mama in Indianapolis, this woman I didn't know, when I was thirteen. She wasn't a hitter, so we got along well. The best part of being with her—after I decided, "Well, I'm not goin' to die living here"—was my baby brother. I came to town on August 6, 1954, and he had been born in June of '54. So he was my puppy. He was mine. I fed him and took care of him. That was the first person that I can remember that loved me. When I was about fourteen, I got a job working weekends to help my mom with whatever I could help her pay. I cooked and waited tables in a restaurant, a fish house on 21st Street.

After I came here, I ran into more prejudice than I did when I was in the South. There were several places—well, most places—that you couldn't go and eat, like Murphy's and Kresge's and Woolworth's. They had little snack bars, but you couldn't go in and sit down. You could order something and take it with you, but you couldn't sit down and eat. It didn't bother me because it was just something that had always happened. This was the way my mom and everybody else did it, and so it didn't bother me that this was going on until people would talk to me about it being wrong. It was just something that came natural.

I had a daughter in 1963. I did what I had to do and started working at a nursing home in the kitchen. There was lots of prejudice there. Many residents didn't want you to touch 'em, but they couldn't do things by themselves. They were old, so we gave them that excuse for being prejudiced. When I went to work, my mother would watch my daughter since we were living with her.

I have a son, too. I got married in 1966, and my boy was born in 1968. After I got married, I had a babysitter for my daughter, and she, some kind of way, let my daughter get burnt. I got to where I didn't trust babysitters anymore. Even though things were hard, I stopped working and stayed at home to be with my children. I did that until my son was in school all day. That's when I started doing day work. It was something that I didn't want to do . . . my mother did it. But that's what I do. I do light cleaning, you know, dusting, mopping, and wiping down appliances. The work doesn't bother me anymore. I've been doing it for more than twenty years.

I raised my children to be nice to each other. They argued when I wasn't around. I know that because it got back to me, but they wasn't allowed to hit each other. They couldn't touch each other. That was a "no-no" at my house. I guess because I was hit as a child, I didn't allow hitting. That hurts. It hurts for someone to take something and hit you with it. You cry, and then they tell you, "I'm really goin' to give you something to cry for." I thought that was one of the meanest things in the world that an adult could say to a child. "I'll hit you, give you pain, and if you don't shut up, I'm goin' to give you more of it."

I'm not married now. I have been separated from my husband since 1988 and divorced for eight years. My ex doesn't help me with anything. I'm by myself. Both my kids have families, and I have nine grandchildren. But I still try to help my children. I don't know how, but the money ends up being there to do it with. I always manage to be able to do a little something because, often they can't afford to do anything without my help. I don't need much. I have learned to live with very little.

Religion plays a big part in my life. There were lots of times that I have attempted to do things that I wanted to do, but God didn't see that it was for me. There was always a reason why it couldn't be done my way. So I had to back up and listen. Every time things seemed like they was just impossible or I couldn't go another day, I'd go in the bathroom—where nobody is lookin' at you—and pray. Then things come out all right.

I mean, I've been praying all my life. I'll be sitting at home by myself, and I say, "Here I am again, God. I know you get tired of hearing from me." I worry Him to death about one thing or another. Sometimes He says, "Hmmm, stupid, you can figure out that one by yourself. You don't need my help." But, other times, I sorta get scared and say, "Ohhhh, I can't do this." But He's there. And then I can do it. You just gotta do it or die . . . and I am not plannin' on goin' no place. I tell my kids I'm goin' to be around to torture them. I'm goin' to be 200 years old, and I'm still goin' to be head of the household.

Interview by Judith Vale Newton

❦

A fifty-seven-year-old African-American, Annie Johnson was born in Atlanta, Georgia. She has two brothers and three sisters, and all but the youngest two were raised by different people. Upon moving to Indianapolis, she attended Indianapolis Public School 1, Indianapolis Public School 17, and Crispus Attucks High School. When she was a senior, she dropped out of school to care for her ailing mother. After Annie's son graduated from high school in 1988, she attended night classes at Broad Ripple High School to obtain her diploma.

They Speak . . . and I Appreciate That

When I was born, I had some vision . . . about 5 percent. I went to a parochial school for a couple of years, and then I came down here from a farm in Starke County to the Indiana School for the Blind. The doctors told me from the time I was small on that I would eventually lose all my central vision . . . the part that determines colors, the part you read with. They said that I would lose my vision completely by the time I was about forty years old. So I knew it was coming, and I tried to prepare for it along the way. Now I have only peripheral vision. I'm aware of light and dark, and I can see shapes of people if I look out the sides of my eyes.

I make my living by selling brooms. I set up at five or six different spots around the north side of Indianapolis, and I try to never stay in the same place more than two days in a row. If it's raining or snowing or bad weather, I go where there's shelter at some of the post offices. And on sunny days, I stay outside and work on the street corners. On any given day, any one of my spots can be a good spot. You know, it's just like anything else when you're involved in sales. You have good days, and you have bad days.

I started making brooms as a craft in high school. They had quite a variety of things you could do as extracurricular activities. Music was one of them. The School for the Blind also taught caning, woodworking, and basket-making. I learned broom-making there. And then, on the weekends, some of us would take these brooms we had made during the week and sell them in the neighborhoods around 75th and Westfield, 75th and College, and on over to the houses on Meridian Street.

When I got out of school, I knew I had to find a means of employment. I went around to different places and filled out a bunch of applications that probably would have been about as thick as a Sears & Roebuck catalogue. All the personnel managers were basically the same. Their bottom line was: "Well, you're a nice guy. We'd love to help you, but. . . ." I decided after that discouraging summer that if I was ever going to make it, I was going to have to do something on my own. I was pretty good at making brooms, so I thought I'd try that venture for a while. I got into it and did pretty well.

I've had to put up with "this, that, and the other thing" through the years. Trying to second-guess the weatherman and determine how to dress is still tough to deal with. Figuring out where I need to be on a given date and trying to pick out an area where I might have a few sales—these things go into my calculations every morning. But, after forty-five years, I've built up a pretty good clientele. About 90 percent of the business I get is either word-of-mouth or repeat customers.

I've learned that people, as a rule, when they see somebody who is different from them or somebody they don't really understand, they're a little bit reserved. It took probably a year or so before anybody started really speaking to me as they'd go by. Even today, I think many folks ignore me because either they don't understand what I'm doing or they don't feel comfortable around somebody like me. I'd say that at each place I work, probably 50 percent of the people at least say "Hi" when they walk by. Some of them have never bought a broom in twenty years, but still, you know, they speak . . . and I appreciate that.

People ask me how I know that my customers are giving me the right money. I guess it is a faith thing for me. The good Lord told me to go out on the street and do His work, and as long as I do it faithfully, He blesses me faithfully. But every once in a while, I do have a problem. In Broad Ripple a couple of weeks ago, a guy walked off with a broom and didn't pay me for it. I thought, "Boy, this is terrible." I got to stewing about it, and finally I looked up and said, "This is Your problem and not mine. I'm not going to worry about it any more." The next day, somebody, an anonymous person, came by and gave me a $100 bill.

You could say my faith is the backbone, the foundation of my life . . . period. You know, they say, "Know the truth, and the truth will set you free." Well, the truth is all in that Book. It's just like if you have an automobile, and that automobile comes equipped with an owner's manual. You can drive that automobile. But somewhere along the line, you're going have questions about that thing, and you have to refer to the owner's manual. The thing of it is, I like the owner's manual of the Guy who designed humanity. So whenever I have any questions or need to be encouraged, I just go to that manual, which is the Bible. With His help, life is exactly what you make of it. Visually handicapped people are as normal as anybody else. We just can't see.

Interview by Judith Vale Newton

Jim Richter is a sixty-four-year-old father of six children. Married to his second wife for eighteen years, he has been selling brooms to passersby in Indianapolis since 1953. Seated on a folding metal chair, in all kinds of weather, Richter is a familiar sight at the post offices in Nora, Broad Ripple, Castleton, and at Bacon Station on 55th Street. He has been functionally blind since birth.

In Vogue

Rosie had just turned twenty-one. I was almost forty-two—twice her age—old enough to be her mother. But she didn't care. All she wanted was someone—anyone—to go out with her. She was on the road to self-discovery—a path I had taken two decades earlier, leaving behind her world of soft drinks and sock hops for a taste of mixed drinks and discos.

But what seemed fresh and exhilarating to her only uncovered faded images for me and stirred up buried emotions. This night meant nothing more to me than dressing up a little for a rare evening on the town, hearing some of my favorite seventies tunes, and checking out the in-crowd. The Vogue was an A-list of people that July 4th night: a news anchor here, a sports celebrity there—a potpourri of professionals.

How excited she was to sample the continuous supply of alcoholic concoctions being delivered to our table, compliments of two overly generous gentlemen sitting nearby. How hopeful she was to be swept off her feet by some dashing prince-of-a-guy, dancing till dawn, only to be whisked away on his beautiful white horse that was tied to a parking meter somewhere along College Avenue.

As we sat for over an hour, on rock-hard bar stools circling a wobbly table, we watched as other women were being asked to dance. One couple after another began filling the dance floor, while impatience was filling Rosie.

"Where are all the guys asking *me* to dance?" Rosie asked. "Is there something wrong with the way I look?"

"Of course not! You look great!" I tried reassuring her. I was curious myself as to why no one approached us. Canvassing the competition, I realized we both were dressed quite differently from the gals who seemed to be having all the fun. They blended into the crowd wearing their micro-mini skirts and tank tops, but we stood out—Rosie in a matronly knee-length dress and me in a conservative pantsuit.

"Maybe we really haven't given anyone a chance to get a good look at us," Rosie remarked. "After all, we're sitting back here in a dark corner. Who can see us? Let's make a trip back to the ladies' room. That's where the lights are the brightest, and there's always a bunch of guys hanging out around there checking out the women coming and going."

"Well, I guess it's worth a try," I responded. "And remember, I'm doing this for you—not me. This isn't my night—it's yours."

As we approached the restroom, we heard—through the standing-room-only crowd—"Too tall!" Following that, someone said, "And the younger one is too fat!" Embarrassed, Rosie shoved open the door, quickened her steps inside to a stall, and wailed that she was not going to come back out.

"Hey, they're just a bunch of drunks. Don't take it so personally, Rosie. What do they know anyway?" I exclaimed, hoping my years of experience and acquired wisdom, though bluntly expressed, could possibly be of some comfort to her.

Finally emerging from her self-imposed exile, Rosie trekked with me back to our waiting table, only to find our stools had been taken by a large party who had moved in while we were out cruising the crowded, smoke-filled room and dodging spilt drinks down our backs—all for the sake of making our presence known.

While standing there at our table feeling foolish, those two generous gentlemen came to our aide offering their own seats. Rosie smiled at me, appearing surprised and even relieved that someone had finally approached us. But soon, insult was added to injury when we discovered at close range that these possible suitors were old enough to be either my father or Rosie's grandfather.

We thanked them for their consideration. Not giving them the opportunity to get to know us better, Rosie asked me, "By the way, what time is it?"

"Eleven o'clock," I responded.

"Well, are you ready to go?" Rosie inquired. "I'm kind of tired."

"Yeah," I said. "I am, too. Ready when you are."

We politely bid adieu to the kind strangers, who appeared upset at our abrupt parting, as if we owed them something for their generosities.

With Rosie leading the way, wearing dashed hopes and a bruised ego on her sleeve, we sheepishly snaked a path to the exit. Little was said between us as we walked down the street toward our welcoming cars, ready to transport us back to the familiar.

Entering the parking lot, we parted ways. As I slid into my car and glanced through the rear view mirror, I caught a glimpse of a man about my age, standing alone—looking about as lonely as I felt.

I turned on the ignition and took another look, finding it hard to take my eyes off this handsome stranger. Was he looking for someone, too? Now *my* mind began to fill with fantasies and my heart raced a little as I imagined the possibilities, but I put my car in gear and drove away, leaving behind the bright lights and promises of Broad Ripple.

Cheryl Soden Moreland

Rocking Babies and Delivering Meals

Thirteen years ago, in September 1986, Tom Gahl (one of our probation officers) was killed. He was the first probation officer ever killed in the line of duty. I don't think there have been any since. He was forty years old. He had two little kids who were four and eight, and his wife was Nancy. I knew Tom because he worked with the court, and I had known him when I was United States attorney. He was really an extraordinarily fine human being. He was involved in the community and was President of his inner-city church (Our Redeemer Lutheran Church).

I wrote a note to Nancy after the funeral to try to express the grief that we all felt. I said, in the way that you do, that if there is anything I can ever do, let me know. Then I got to thinking that was really a hollow gesture because Nancy was not going to call me up. So I decided I should call her. I asked her if she wanted to have lunch. It turned out in our conversation over lunch that we had known each other as children. We used to play together when we were preschoolers.

We have developed a really great friendship since then. Since Tom was killed, every year on the anniversary of his death (September 22), Nancy and I have done something in the early morning hours of that sad day to take us outside of ourselves, to move our minds from the sadness of the past to the future, and in particular, to think of the people and things beautiful that are all around us.

As a federal probation officer, Tom had been very active and involved in the community and in the lives of the people he supervised. Many of those people had lots of problems to contend with just to get along from day to day. We decided we wanted to do something that, in some way, continued his legacy and influence for good in the community. We have shared these observances now for more than thirteen years.

The first year, we met at Nancy's church, where she and Tom had been very active. We drove back to the scene of the shooting. We stood there and talked for a while, and Nancy left a rose in Tom's memory. Afterward, we were given a very special tour of Methodist Hospital by then President Frank Lloyd, followed by lunch.

In subsequent years, we have spent special mornings rocking babies in the extended care section of the newborn unit at Methodist. We have delivered meals for Meals-on-Wheels and helped to serve lunch at the Dayspring Shelter. We have planted bulbs in Nancy's yard to come up in the spring; we have made baskets at the kitchen table of a friend and taken long, autumn walks in the country.

Once, we found out that Methodist Hospital offered literacy classes for its employees. We thought we might be of some help, giving encouragement and support. We were just going to audit the class. There were six students, and we obviously didn't belong. The teacher introduced us and asked if I would tell the class about the courts and my work. I said I would, but asked if the students would tell me about themselves first.

It was a roomful of talkers. About forty-five minutes later, they had all told Nancy and me about themselves. They told stories of great persistence and courage in overcoming lots of obstacles that the rest of us haven't had to face in our lives.

The only man in the class was a guy named James who had gone to Arsenal Technical High School in Indianapolis. He was in his early forties. When it came time for him to tell about his life and experiences, he told about having been an athlete at Tech. He got pushed along from class to class because of his athletic prowess. Finally, by about ninth grade, he couldn't keep up any more. He dropped out of school and he got married right away. His girlfriend was pregnant. He had to get a job. One of his problems was that he hadn't learned to read. He was pushed into the workforce to support himself and his family right away. He always had entry level, menial jobs that allowed him to get by without knowing how to read.

He had been working at Methodist for awhile. He raised his kids and decided he wanted to learn how to read. This had always held him back, and he wanted the opportunity to go farther in life, to have a more fulfilling life. When he was telling the story, he said, "I'm going to do it, too. I'm moving out of the darkness; I can see the light."

Nancy and I thought that was reason enough to have gone there that day, to hear him say that.

Interview by Sandy Sasso

※

Sarah Evans Barker is Chief Judge, United States District Court, Southern District of Indiana. She grew up in Mishawaka, Indiana.

Being Forgiven Gives You **Lots of Freedom**

It was January 1978, the time of the great blizzard. I was a fifteen-year-old sophomore in high school, shoveling snow in our driveway with my father, Adam Streett. Two men came up behind us. "Don't move," one of them said. "Nobody will get hurt." When we turned around and my father asked, "What's going on here?" one of the men, whose name was Michael Daniels, shot him through the heart.

Seventeen years later, I was working as a minister in inner-city Chicago, trying to get some folks employed in the neighborhood. My wife and I were living in a predominantly black community and worshipping in a predominantly African-American church. As white people, we were dealing with those relationships and cultural differences. Yet I was still harboring some bitterness toward the black man who killed my father, and I think that extended towards black people in general. I think that it was my attempt to deal with the situation—to deal with the fact that the world was telling me that I should be bitter and angry, and I should not forgive.

The Gospel message is quite the opposite. I've always tried to do what God told me to do. He told me to work and live in a black community. But really,

I had not been able to take that one step further, to really forgive the man who killed my father.

I finally did that, in a letter to Michael Daniels in the Indiana State Prison. I never heard back from him.

After I moved back to Indianapolis, I was having lunch with a black minister friend when the story of Michael Daniels came up. My friend mentioned that he knew Don Cox, the man who drove the car in the robbery. He also told me that Don had become a Christian while in the Indiana Reformatory at Pendleton. So I wrote basically the same letter to Don that I had written to Michael, forgiving him and asking him if I could come see him sometime. He wrote back immediately, and said that he'd love to have me come up.

We were together for about an hour that first meeting. He had the opportunity to express to me his repentance, and he said how sorry he was for what happened. He was not making excuses but was taking full responsibility. I told him that I forgave him. I gave him some messages from my family, saying the same thing. I think it was a very healing time for both of us.

I know that it was healing time for him, because there is something powerful about forgiveness, which I am just learning. Being forgiven gives you lots of freedom. I think Don began to express that freedom, freedom to grow and to put his past behind him. He'd been very arrogant, not caring about what he had done over the years. I think that God worked on his heart, and he began to realize what he had done to me and to our family.

Our being together released him from the burden he'd been carrying. I knew that I did not want it to be just one time, and so I asked him if I could come see him again. He said he'd love that. He asked me if I would speak to his family, to his mother. He told me he'd write to me and give me his mother's phone number. The very next night, even before I had a chance to get a letter from him, his sister called. She said, "So, I just got off from the phone with Don, and he told me that you went to visit him." She expressed how happy she was about that, and I suggested we get together for dinner. At my wife's urging, we ended up having dinner at our house with Don's mother, Jayne Beckett, two of his sisters, and a brother. We had a really nice time. We really hit it off. They told me how sorry they were that a member of their family had done this.

It was interesting, because Don had maintained his innocence for fifteen years, and they'd believed him. It was only about two years before our dinner together that he told them he really had been involved. So the family was dealing with lots of emotions, too. They'd had to deal with the bitterness against the system, the police, the prosecutor. Then, when he confessed to them, they had to deal with their feelings toward his lying and his crime. Obviously, they had to give up all the bitterness they had for the people they thought had ruined their brother. It was a good time for them as well as for us.

We've kept up the relationships. I have been to prison to visit Don on several occasions. We write to each other consistently. He is much better at writing than I am. He jokes that he has more time on his hands. We talk on the phone, probably once a month. My family continues to have dinner with his family. When our new baby was born, they came over and brought him a gift.

Interview by Hande Birkalan

❧

Tim Streett is a husband, a father, and a resident of the Martindale-Brightwood neighborhood of Indianapolis. Tim serves as Minister of Urban Outreach for the East 91st Street Christian Church in Indianapolis. Jireh Sports, an after-school recreation and tutoring program, has grown out of 91st Street's partnership with seven different inner-city churches in the Martindale-Brightwood Community.

the place
where you
stand is holy

City stories are grounded in place; they unfold on the avenues, playing fields, gardens, and homes that make up the landscape of a particular urban center. Understanding a city's geography requires more than a map of its topography. A city is the monuments and museums people come to visit and the sanctuaries they seek to get away from it all. It is defined as much by its renovated historic district and its newly constructed city center as it is by its trailer parks and decaying neighborhoods. Some locations memorialize events and preserve the past, and new structures concretize present realities and imagine the future.

We look at places through different lenses. What is for one person a beltway representing convenience is for another disturbance, an intrusion into the character of a community. What for many is construction that symbolizes progress is for others disruption and loss of home.

The stories in this section ask us to look at the landmarks and gathering places of Indianapolis—from the small cafés where one can linger over coffee while poets read their works to the race track where fried chicken mixes with speeding cars. These stories take us up and down Meridian Street and onto the highways that circle and intersect the city.

In the book of Genesis, the patriarch Jacob flees from Beersheba to escape the wrath of his brother, Esau. On his journey he comes upon a certain place and spends the night there. Using a stone as a pillow, he falls asleep. He dreams of a ladder with its top in the sky and with angels of God going up and down it. When Jacob awakes he says, "Surely God is in this place and I did not know it. . . . How awesome is this place! This is none other than the abode of God and that is the gateway to heaven" (Genesis 28:17). He called the city Bethel, the house of God.

One might expect the angels on Jacob's ladder to be descending and ascending rather than the reverse. Perhaps the sacred begins not in the heavens, not even in the sanctuaries meant to serve as houses of God, but in the many structures where we live and work, the places we congregate to distract us and to help us remember. In the stories that follow, you will meet the angels ascending.

Remove the shoes from your feet
because the place where you stand is holy.

—Exodus 3:5

At the Track

It's race day again, and Steve wheels his Harley out of the garage. It's the best way to get to the track, weaving in and out of bumper-to-bumper traffic, riding the shoulder of the road, cutting across mall parking lots. With our friends, Sid and Pam on Sid's Harley, we pass cars with their windows up, passengers breathing in the last cool air they'll feel for awhile, and pickup trucks with beds full of race fans, already drinking beer. Music, mostly rock and roll, spills out into the May morning. Near Speedway, the streets narrow. The front yards of nearly all the small tract houses near the track are full of parked cars and motorcycles. At twenty bucks a pop, residents can earn a tidy sum on race day. Few spend the money for race tickets, though. They sit outside on lawn chairs, watch the crazy race fans go by, and listen to the race on the radio.

A woman who lives in Speedway once told me that her family took shifts staying up the night before the race. They had to, she said, to keep the drunks from peeing on her peonies. The inebriated fans would finally pass out around dawn, and she took particular pleasure when they were shocked awake around seven, by the Speedway High School band. The kids marched from the high school to the track, playing "America the Beautiful" along the way.

"Ten bucks for a motorcycle," a guy hollers from the sidewalk. "Nice shady spot."

"Deal," Steve says. We pull in, park, hang our helmets on the handlebars, and join the parade of people heading for the track.

I love the sound of ice rattling in the heavy coolers, the smell of suntan lotion, the little kids wearing too-big Pennzoil or Pep Boys baseball caps and t-shirts with race cars on them. There are college students with yin-yang tattoos or tattooed Grateful Dead teddy bears dancing around their ankles and rednecks with big-breasted ladies tattooed on their biceps. A girl in short-shorts, with a patch on one pocket that says "Don't Be a Dick" flounces past a down-and-out looking guy holding a hand-lettered sign that says, "*Isn't It Time for Jesus?*"

We have great seats, high up in the third turn. We can see the line of pace cars carrying the 500 Festival queen and her princesses as they come along the backstretch, through the short-chute, and into the fourth turn. Then come the "celebrities," a motley crew of politicians and sit-com stars. The Goodyear blimp floats above us; helicopters circle. Across the track, in the infield, race fans are in constant motion: walking, bicycling, playing Frisbee. They lounge on blankets and lawn chairs, on car roofs, and in the beds of pickup trucks.

Vast video screens dot the infield, facing the stands. Advertisements for every kind of automotive product give way to still images of the American flag. These dissolve into black and white film footage of the D-Day landing. Suddenly, there's an odd whooshing sound and a stealth bomber appears on the horizon. It is black, bat-like, flat as a landing field. The crowd roars as it thunders over us, exhilarated by its sheer power; but I'm struck with real fear, because I can't help imagining what it must be like to see this killing machine appear, armed with real bombs meant for destruction.

There's little time to ponder this, though. CeCe Wynans appears on the video screens and renders an extraordinary version of "The Star-Spangled Banner." Then there's my favorite race moment: Jim Nabors singing "Back Home Again in Indiana" and thousands of colorful balloons let loose into the summer sky.

"Gentlemen, start your engines."

One by one the cars start up, screaming, and soon they appear behind the pace car on the backstretch, wavering in the heat. The crowd rises, shouting, waving as they pass. They take a second turn around the track, the drivers swerving slightly to break in their tires. Then the green flag falls on the front stretch and the race begins.

The cars zoom past. Again. Again. They go past so quickly that I can barely read the numbers on them; then soon the faster drivers lap the slower ones, so I have no idea by looking who's doing well or poorly. Like most people around me, I listen to the race on a Walkman radio, the voices of the broadcast broken by static adding to the scream of the engines on the track.

I'm good for maybe fifty laps, then my attention flags and I graze in the picnic cooler we've brought. Ham sandwiches, potato chips, deviled eggs, Mint Milano cookies. In fact, there's food everywhere I look—fried chicken, potato salad, cole slaw, hot dogs, French fries, ice cream bars, nachos and cheese, carrot sticks, cupcakes, pasta salad, apples, bananas, red licorice, sushi. Across the track, in the infield, people are cooking on hibachis, the smoke curling up into the sky. Through the binoculars, I watch some kind of altercation flare up near a battered pickup truck with Q95 painted on the roof, but it doesn't last long. Four motorcycle cops appear on the scene, and pretty soon all the guys who were fighting are looking at the bikes, including a shirtless fat man wearing a red plastic racing helmet and yellow goggles.

There's a crash in the first turn, and the yellow light goes on. The cars go by at a mere hundred or so miles an hour now, and we pass the time by taking advantage of the reduced roar to share race stories. Steve's been going to the race since he was a little boy. In fact, his birthday is May 30, and for the longest time, his dad let him believe the race was run for him. He saw the driver Eddie Sachs burn to death in front of him; he was there when Parnelli Jones's turbo engine—the first to run at the 500—gave out in the last lap. We remember sitting in the paddock together in the late sixties when corporations hired black bartenders to serve their blocs of well-dressed executives and guests. There were the infield years, too—when our brother-in-law practiced carrying his full cooler the night before the race, and the time a few years ago, when my English mother's cousin came from his home in Sweden to see the race and they reconnected for the first time since the War.

"I was mistaken for Janet Guthrie in the garage area, the first year she drove," I say. "For me, that was the high point! The low point was going with Steve's clients, who owned a chicken processing plant and had *Eat More Chicken* written in huge letters on the side of their car. They did, too. Eat more chicken, I mean. My God, I've never seen so much chicken in my whole life! Then, after the race, the guy stopped the car in the middle of horrible traffic and sent his wife into Steak and Shake to buy a bag of hamburgers to tide them over on the trip back to Broad Ripple."

Pam tells about the time she made flashcards for each car, hoping for once to keep track of what was going on.

"Did it work?" I ask.

"No," she says. "I still didn't have a clue."

Shortly after that, the two of us take a break to check out the gift shop. There are the predictable t-shirts, baseball caps, and model cars. We also find hair accoutrements, baseballs, whiskey glasses, golf balls, magnets, belt buckles, spoons, key chains, stadium seats, lighters, Christmas ornaments, baby socks, and earrings—all with the official 500 insignia. I buy a *Welcome Race Fans* banner for our front porch, chatting with the sales clerk who rings up the sale. She had to be there at four a.m., she tells me. Tyce Carlson, a driver, walked to the track from his house in Speedway at six.

"Does business ever slow down in here?" I ask.

She shrugs. "Sometimes. Then there'll be a crash, and it's packed again."

Back in the stands, we eat some more. The race goes on. When I look at the big electronic statistics board in the infield now, it's to calculate how many laps are left. I'm hot, tired, bordering on crabby. This is it, I say to myself. I hate this stupid race. I'm never coming back.

But I know I will.

Barbara Shoup

Statuary in Rather **Grotesque Positions**

It's an odd thing, the monument. Thousands of pounds of limestone with brass and copper overlays standing there pointing at the sky, statuary in rather grotesque positions all around it gasping and dying, and serene fountains in front looking rather out of place with all this Civil War imagery.

Some people have made fun of it, scorning it even from the first days when Colonel Lew Wallace insisted that he was resigning from the Monument Building commission because "no woman ought to be put up on top of that thing."

But it's a little like us in Indianapolis—us Indianapolitans or whatever it is you call folks who inhabit this city. Look deeper at the thing, and you see who we are in this city or the state for that matter. These are the faces of thousands of eighteen- and twenty-year-olds who fought and died at Antietam and Vicksburg and Gettysburg. My own great-grandfather was here to dedicate this hulking obelisk in 1905; he was twenty when he took a bullet at the Wilderness.

We're patriotic, unabashedly so. Our state sent the second highest total of men for our population to the Northern war effort.

We're persistent, stubborn some might say. The Civil War soldiers used to say in their letters, "We're going to stay 'til this thing is done, fight whatever battles they throw at us, because that's the way we do things back home in Indianney." It took twelve years to build the Monument, and several times, they thought they wouldn't get it done.

We know how to survive, too. We transformed most of the shabby, old area around the Circle into the Circle Centre Mall; we polished up the brass on the monument itself and made a fine Civil War museum in its basement. An average of three thousand people go through that museum each weekend to learn why we fought to the death to free the slaves and save the Union.

Well, if it is a little clunky or a bit corny, so are we. We have our palaces of art, but we still are pretty down to earth. We try to solve our problems, we work, we raise our children in values of the countryside.

Our downtown went way down twenty years ago, but we rallied as a city and rebuilt it resplendently. We don't take failure easily in Indianapolis. After all, that's Miss Victory up on top of the Monument, isn't it?

Nancy Niblack Baxter

Leg Squats in Evening Clothes

Fireworks illuminate the night sky. Strolling musicians, stilt walkers, and jugglers mingle with—and captivate—the crowd. So do half a dozen Broadway and Hollywood celebrities.

More than five thousand Hoosiers have paid $100 each to attend this black-tie celebration in the heart of downtown Indianapolis. A Queen Elizabeth imperson-ator decked out in a glittering tiara, gloves, and a floor-length gown greets guests on the third floor of Circle Centre, the crown jewel of a resurgent downtown.

The real question isn't why so many Hoosiers—including me, a journalist covering the gala for *The Indianapolis Star*—have donned formal attire on this joyous evening in September 1995. The real question is why make such a fuss over a shopping mall?

Well, it's like this: Circle Centre is a symbol of something greater—albeit a spectacular symbol with its atriums, skylines, Artsgarden, chic restaurants, and banks of escalators.

When I was growing up here in the sixties and seventies, my hometown was known as Naptown or, worse, India-NO-PLACE. Downtown had a hum to it, but barely. And its hum mostly was confined to the holiday season. My treasured memories include trips with my grandmother to visit Santa and eat lunch at the L. S. Ayres Tea Room, the purveyor of the world's best chicken velvet soup.

Other than those Yuletide adventures and occasional trips to our parents' offices, suburban kids like me almost never visited downtown. By the way, I considered myself a "suburban" kid even though my family lived in Warren Township, well within Marion County.

Those of us in the townships—whether Warren, Washington, Pike, Wayne, or Perry—didn't feel part of a thriving urban community. Why would we? The city didn't have a pulsating center, or heart.

But on this evening at Circle Centre in 1995, the buzz is about a pulsating downtown. Its revival speeded up in the eighties, shifting into high gear with the move of a professional football team, the Baltimore-turned-Indianapolis Colts.

Next came a flurry of activity, including the opening of cultural gems like the Eiteljorg Museum of American Indian and Western Art, as well as the flourishing of downtown neighborhoods.

But back to the festivities at Circle Centre's grand opening. People are almost giddy in their sense of civic spirit. I can't help grinning at a seventy-two-year-old businessman who—despite his tuxedo, cummerbund, and black leather shoes—is straddling exercise equipment in a newly opened fitness store. He's doing leg squats in his evening clothes!

"I just had to sample the merchandise," he tells me.

Even the comedians aren't poking fun at the former *India-no-place.* Take my buddy Wil Shriner, a standup comic and TV personality.

He's the son of Herb Shriner, a long-gone, beloved entertainer who became nationally famous as the "Hoosier Humorist" during the fifties—right about the time Indy was nodding off on the road to Naptown.

"I've been coming to this city since I was a little kid," says Wil, who grew up in southern California.

As we chat, more fireworks explode over our heads—and hundreds of Hoosiers applaud a performance by Grammy Award-winning singer Sandi Patty. She's just belted out a rousing version of a song titled "Indianapolis, Indeed!"

Wil's voice softens as he steps to a microphone and tells the audience of Indianapolis residents: "My dad would be so proud to see what you have done here."

Nelson Price

Echoes

It's not like I can't see the glory of the new downtown. Like anyone else, I can walk the freshly-poured sidewalks past the elegant Parisian and the retro-cool Conseco Fieldhouse, or stroll under the spectacular Artsgarden toward the party at the Hard Rock Cafe. I can admire the newly-masoned brick and stone facades of the historic apartment buildings, and I can see the smiling out-of-towners filing into Circle Centre Mall. I've watched the ribbon-cutting ceremonies celebrating the rebirth, revitalization, reinvigoration, regeneration of our city center.

I can see the glory of the new downtown. I just can't hear it. Sure, there are the sounds of ice cubes tinkling in Palomino's glasses, wardrobe decisions being debated at Nordstrom's, and loud laughter from Alcatraz Brewing Company. Everywhere there are sounds of credit cards and bar codes being swiped through electronic readers. But for me, the sound of the new downtown is muddled by echoes from the old downtown it displaced.

Echoes of soft conversations with a family I knew who lived at the Lionel Artis on North Meridian, three generations of African-American women together for decades in a public housing building filled with cousins and aunts and lifelong friends. Echoes of the frail voice of Mary Hanshew, an elderly woman who lived with her brother in the Hoosier Apartments on Massachusetts Avenue. Echoes of homeless men bringing their troubles to the doctors and lawyers and social workers who served them at Horizon House.

I stopped by the Lionel Artis the other day, but the family I knew was long gone. Along with hundreds of other poor people whose subsidized housing buildings were shut down and sold off to developers, they had to leave downtown. The Lionel Artis is now The Continental, and the cheery red-haired leasing agent is willing to show me two-bedroom apartments that start at $1,000 a month. She hands me a brochure that includes a map showing The Continental's proximity to the Indiana Repertory Theatre, the Indianapolis Symphony Orchestra, and "a variety of shopping centers."

Mary Hanshew's building was sold off, too. She found another apartment north of downtown, but unlike the Hoosier, it is not within walking distance to the grocery store and the pharmacy. She's seventy-nine, and her brother passed away last year. She has to ask for rides from other people to run her errands, and she fears this dependence will soon land her in a nursing home.

The low-income Hoosier Apartments building that she called home is now the Davlan Building, and after renovations, it will be taking in new tenants. Mary Hanshew won't be one of them, though. "I hear they are going to charge at least $600 a month. That's more than my entire Social Security check," she says with a sour laugh. Then her voice goes lower and she looks away. "I can't think of any place downtown that I can afford now."

Horizon House isn't around anymore, either. For ten years, the agency served as a day center for the city's homeless, a place to pick up mail, take a shower, get some help filling out a rental application. Then Horizon House lost its lease for its Washington Street home and had to move. New locations were found, grants were awarded, contracts were signed. But one after another, three different plans to move to downtown locations were blocked by zoning boards, neighborhood associations, and city-county councilors. "We know that Horizon House provides a vital service," one neighborhood association leader told me. "It's just that those services attract these homeless people into the area."

Eventually, the lease ran out and with no place left to go, Horizon House just shut down. So did the downtown Food Stamps office on South Meridian

Street, replaced by Jillian's Video Café, Bar, and Hibachi Grill. On the well-lit sidewalks, a new anti-panhandling law is being enforced. The downtown bus stops have been moved away from the high-traffic shopping areas.

But I still hear the echoes, like the last sound that came from Horizon House. At the end of a small closing ceremony, someone strummed an acoustic guitar while homeless people and social workers linked arms and sang, some with tears streaming down their faces. They sang the classic Woody Guthrie anthem.

"This land is your land, this land is my land. This land belongs to you and me."

They sang it straight, no irony. But when I hear their voices in the new downtown, the words sound hollow, as echoes sometimes do.

Fran Quigley

One of the Great **Town Avenues in America**

T onight I think that this is my town, Indianapolis. Mine, and thousands of others who are heading down Meridian Street to see the Christmas lights on Monument Circle.

I am struck by the beauty of the night and by my feelings of ownership of this street, famous in the nation as one of the great town avenues in America. Why is it, I ask myself, that when I turn onto this six-mile strip of macadam that I feel such a sense of satisfaction, even ownership? There's a comfort level in being "on Meridian" that ranges somewhere between getting an A on a test and receiving a mug of hot chocolate from Mom on a blustery day.

Perhaps it is the layers of memories that inhabit the street, casting long shadows, joining the *then* and *now*. In that house on the west side, our engagement was announced. There, near 46th Street, I walked from my nearby school to a friend's house along a particularly beautiful mile. Here, right here, as we drove by in our 1948 Chevrolet, is where Booth Tarkington lived, my dad had said. And there, at that house near 38th Street, we stopped to see Tom Joyce's house. He dazzled the town with his enormous display of decorations at a time when the city was just recovering from the War.

Of course it is a historical street. But its culmination—there, in the Mile Square as I explain to my grandchildren, are places whose history reaches beyond my own. There is the neoclassical Indianapolis public library, proudly opened as a city cultural landmark in 1916, where generations of us have browsed the open stacks for term papers and learned a little about architectural grandeur. There are the Scottish Rite cathedral, a miracle of a depression-age civic effort, and classy office buildings of the city's seventies rebirth, on the site of older office buildings. All of them wear a Christmas face.

I don't think it's the street itself that has the most fascination for me. Maybe it's the Circle itself. Here, as a pre-teen, I used to wander with friends to the Circle Theatre. Then past the delicately beautiful Christ Church, which as one of the oldest in the city has seen the governor's mansion of past days, the Civil War, anxious war brides kneeling to pray in its aisles as the Normandy Invasion began. We all live in a time warp that our historical buildings and streets create for us, though we do not know it.

No, I finally realize as I look up at the tent of lights that has transformed the Circle's center into a Christmas tree, it is the Monument itself, visible down Meridian Street for many blocks, that I love most, that bonds me to this street most of all.

Nancy Niblack Baxter

Another Car **Pulled Up**

It was one of those warm summer afternoons with that special light that makes you feel glad to be alive. Cars were moving in unison out of the parking garages, away from work, toward home. I turned my car east on Ohio Street and was again struck by the apparent narrowness of the street. It is as wide as any other Indianapolis street, but with the tallest of the city's buildings lining it, and the constant waddling of Indy-Go buses over the drainage inlets in the outer lanes, it seems to cut a narrow path through the densest part of the city. Today, seeing this scene again, I flashed on the memory of when I first noticed it several years ago, and I also remembered having a sense of pride that I was a small part of this huge enterprise. I turned my view to my right, toward the Statehouse, and noticed the people waiting at the corner bus stop. Two women were laughing as they held babies in their arms. It was a perfect day.

I first noticed him on the sidewalk before he even set foot in the street. There was something about him that made me pay attention. It was the walk. Yes, it was his walk. He was a tall, good-looking black man, perhaps in his mid-twenties. He was happy. That stroll was such that no white man could imitate it without looking silly, but it fit him perfectly. It was the proud gait that betrayed his enjoyment of a beautiful day.

My car was in the center lane, and I had not noticed that another car had pulled up on my right. The black man had stepped into the street and was just starting to pass in front of the car next to me when I heard it. It was the audibly loud click of electric door locks from the car next to me. If it had been a cooler day, I would not have heard it. Everyone, it seemed, had car windows down. The click of those locks intruded on my thoughts and those of the black man as well. I knew he had heard them. I saw him change—not significantly, but something happened to him. It was more of a mental change than a physical one. It seemed confined to his face. He looked neither at me nor at the car to my right. He just kept going. But he had changed. I could feel it.

As he passed my car and proceeded to the sidewalk on the far side of Ohio Street, I glanced to my right to see who had locked the doors. It was a woman of about fifty wearing a blond wig in a large car. She was looking right at me with a look that said she realized what she had just done. Our eyes met but for a moment, and then she lowered hers and faced forward. Maybe seven seconds had passed since I first noticed the man.

As the light turned green, I shot a look at the man's back, but noticed nothing, and out of the corner of my eye I saw the car with the woman in the wig start to turn right. I looked ahead of my car and took my foot off the brake. We left in opposite directions.

Kim Charles Ferrill

Whack!

Whack! went the baseball bat, the weapon of choice. Whack! Whack! Again and again. One person after another, taking turns. How long would it take?

What was once a rainbow-hued star that swung way above their little heads, suspended from atop a tall ladder, was now reduced to nothing more than a shattered shell, always the fate of a battered piñata.

I watched as a very small girl, with eyes as big as they were brown, knelt to inspect what relics lay before her. In a corner, Latin rhythms blared from a borrowed boom box, unable to compete with the shrieks of triumph from the children with full fists greedily eager to take pieces of the action home with them to flaunt and to hoard.

This was not the Fountain Square that I remembered, not the place where I grew up. I wasn't accustomed to seeing this many people of color in my neighborhood, nor had I ever witnessed an incident such as this. So much cheering and revelry was going on around me that the noise was almost deafening. And most of the time I couldn't understand what was being said. Their language was foreign to me and to several locals who had gathered to witness the joyful mayhem.

During my childhood years, I had become familiar with Italian accents as I played in those southeast-side streets and the brogue of the Irish as they gossiped in the graveled alleys. But I was never introduced to the Mexican dialect.

That night, the camaraderie of the participants was evident in their smiles and their laughter, and in the coming-together of races and ages that I hadn't seen before near my childhood home. Friends. Amigos. Brothers.

All this joy was stemming from one rather simple event hosted by Fountain Square's small library for the good of the community, aptly called *Fiesta*!

As sad as it had been over the years to watch as the original inhabitants and immigrants of Fountain Square slowly fade away, it was exciting and hopeful to experience this new ethnicity being added to a community whose racial diversity had been dwindling.

How times had changed. How people had changed. This was not the Fountain Square that I remembered. This was better.

Cheryl Soden Moreland

Making Sense of a **Flower Bed**

When I first moved to Indianapolis, I lived with a friend (also recently transplanted here) in a house she bought in the Meridian/Kessler area. The large yard surrounding the house had been neglected, according to neighbors, for about sixteen years. So we found ourselves weeding flowerbeds, pruning trees and bushes, and planting, which kept us outside frequently.

One evening while we were out, a neighbor stopped by after work to talk. While she was there, another woman came by. We discovered that all the neighbors directly around us were single women. "Let's have a neighborhood pitch-in!" one of the women said. "We'll introduce you." The women at the pitch-in gave us advice about house maintenance. "Don't try to cut corners to save money," they warned. One told how she had tried to fix her driveway herself by patching it with cement and had made such a mess that she had to have it completely removed and redone. Another told about her experience hiring a carpenter to build kitchen cabinets. His bid had been the lowest. She gave him her house key so he could work during the day while she was at the office. One night at twelve o'clock, she woke up to hear him hammering away in the kitchen. "Ask us," they said, "if you need information about house repairs." They also told us the best places to go for ice cream or Chinese take-out. They helped us feel less strange and new.

Three months after I moved into my friend's house, my mother unexpectedly died. Because of the suddenness and the mystery surrounding it, her death shattered me. She died at her doctor's office after a routine test about which she had told no family members. We had not even known she wasn't feeling well. I felt devastated and guilty. Why hadn't she told us? If she had, could we have prevented her death?

To escape the pain and self-incrimination, I worked more frequently on the yard. My heart stunned, I felt best when I had something tangible to do with my hands. I chopped away at bushes that had overrun the driveway and lopped off tree branches that hung too far over the sidewalk. I dug around the scraggly flowers in the weedy flowerbeds. I found comfort planting Sweet Williams and watching the world around me falling into order and flourishing under my care.

Working outside in the yard helped me meet more neighbors. One Saturday afternoon as I chopped down a large bush that looked like a decrepit, overgrown yak, the couple from across the street strolled by with their two young children. "Looking good," the wife nodded. "Big improvement." She told me that the large bush had been the favorite hiding place for cops trying to nab speeders on Riverview Drive. While we talked, their children played happily on my front lawn. I found out that the husband had requested the stop sign the city put in front of my house because he was concerned about the safety of children with so many cars speeding on Riverview Drive. He was also involved in the White River Greenway Project and said that a proposed path along the river was being blocked by our neighbors. The conversation traveled to other areas—The Sierra Club and the Indianapolis Traditional Music and Dance Group. I found we knew many of the same people. Little by little, I learned about the neighborhood from those who stopped to admire the garden.

Another evening while I was trying to make sense of a flowerbed that seemed to be mostly a tangle of vines, rocks, and a few dying rosebushes, Susan, who lived kitty-corner from us, brought over two large Coreopsis plants left over from planting. "Here," she said. "I've got a couple too many. You take them." Planted beside the rosebushes, they blossomed all summer and into the fall, bright spots of yellow that greeted me when I drove up each evening after work.

We soon discovered that this was a neighborhood where people walked. Each evening people walked by our house on the corner: single persons, couples, and families. Sometimes, people from blocks away would stop and compliment us on our yard work and then stay to talk. I admit that sometimes getting the gardening done was hard, but those people stopping by to talk sustained me during a difficult time. In the six months after my mother died, I found myself traveling every other week to Minnesota to help my father adjust to my mother's death. Because I had just moved to Indianapolis, I didn't know many people besides Nancy, my housemate and also from Minnesota. Having these people stop to talk gave me much needed contact with people outside of my job.

Also during this time, I was working on a project researching atrocities committed by U.S. troops during the Vietnam War. The horror of the accounts I read sometimes just would not leave me. So people stopping by to talk gave me back some faith in people that I'd lost because of what I'd read. Their small acts of kindness and hospitality helped me. I wish they could have known. We stood outside and talked about how to care for the roses or which flowers took the least amount of care—basic facts.

After about a year and a half, I bought a condo near Eagle Creek Park on the outer edges of Indianapolis. I don't have a garden anymore; in fact, none of my neighbors have gardens. I've lived here a year now, and even though there are more people per square mile where I now live, I know fewer people. I don't talk to many of my neighbors on a daily basis as I once did. Last weekend when a friend came over for dinner, he remarked, "Where are all the people who live here hiding?" I laughed. But when I looked out, the street in front of my condo did seem deserted. Around the area in front where visitors park their cars are about sixteen condos, each with an average of two people. But no one was to be seen. On the quarter-mile-long lane to my driveway stand about sixty condos, but on any given evening after work, I may see only one or two people out walking. In the year since I moved, I've talked to maybe three of my neighbors at any length. I was here six months before I met anyone. People are either in their homes or in their cars going somewhere.

Elizabeth Weber

Hungry to See Live Theatre

I climb up the winding staircase to the cavernous lobby of the Athenaeum Turner's building on Michigan Street. It is 1975, and I am six months pregnant. It is a winter opening night at the Indiana Repertory Theatre. Instead of acting, I am house managing. My last performance as Candy Starr, the little prostitute who visits asylum inmate McMurphy in *One Flew Over the Cuckoo's Nest* was two months ago. Near the end of the run, after having graduated into roomier jeans for the part, I am teased by my fellow actors. "Every night at nine o'clock sharp, that little kid is gonna jump up with a start, and never know the reason why," they say. That's the approximate time that I used to jump from a window into McMurphy's arms in the second act. Now I stand by the doors to the auditorium and pass out programs. "Good evening, please go to your left; hope you enjoy the show." I am wearing a bright red velour dressing gown that I think passes for eveningwear. It's the only thing I own that will accommodate my growing stomach.

It's fun to be on this side of things. I had no idea how hungry this audience is to see live theatre. Now I can see it on their faces. They crowd forward, eager to plant themselves in their seats and devour the program. Some of them remember me from *Cuckoo's Nest* and smile. Some wish me luck and ask when I'm due.

My husband, Richard, and I have been here exactly one year. He arrived first to take on the job of Resident Scene Designer for IRT's second season. I finished up acting and teaching in Kansas City at the Missouri Repertory Theatre, and then joined him. I auditioned for Ed Stern, IRT's Artistic Director, and he cast me in the season's opener: *Harvey.* To make extra money, Richard took on a job painting the basement of Sam's Subway, a popular restaurant behind the Marott Hotel, to actually look like a subway. My contribution was to paint the people riding on the train. While working on this mural, I stopped to place a call to the nurse at my OB-GYN's office and found out that I was pregnant. I remember staring at the cartoon faces I'd drawn and thinking, "Time, as we know it, has stopped."

We never meant to stay. Life was going to be nomadic for us. We had been warned by our theatre professors, "You'll never be hired at the same theatre at the same time: So don't expect it." Indianapolis was just another stop in our grand plan to work in regional theatre. Who needed New York City?

Theatre was booming in the heartland, with new plays being written, strong companies being formed, and great facilities being built. And look at India-no-place for crying out loud. The downtown was deader than dead after five o'clock on any weekday, and the weekends made it a ghost town.

Our apartment is in the back of this building. After rehearsal or after a show, Richard and I go down to the Rathskeller in the basement and wind through the tables of customers eating bratwurst and sauerkraut to the back of the restaurant. A door opens onto the Beer Garden—a huge walled-in space for summer dances and pig roasts. The back door of our apartment is a hundred yards from the outdoor stage on which the Athenaeum Turner's Band plays every Saturday night in the summer. Japanese lanterns hang, like a necklace of orange and yellow baubles, on the high wall all year round. Inside, our living room has huge timbers traversing the ceiling, and our second-floor bedroom window looks out onto a front gated garden. Here Tanker, our basset hound, sticks his nose through the iron grating and receives pats and treats from the homeless folk in the early hours of the morning.

We pick up their trash that blows into the yard, especially on weekends. On weekdays, we can sit on the small cement slab of a porch and not be seen by passersby on their way to work. The men sport white buck shoes in the summer, and the women often wear hats.

Inside these walls, my husband designs a lavish Southern parlor for Regina in Lillian Hellman's *Little Foxes.* He works in the same room that will soon belong to our baby. I busy myself with making curtains and completing a needlepoint picture of Peter Rabbit.

Three months later, Sarah is born. She is a phenomenon for the theatre staff, because most of them are not even married. They stare at her, and she stares back with equal seriousness. We nickname her Winston Churchill. She consumes my summer, and I begin to think that acting is over for me. I've started doing some commercial work, and that seems like a possible career move. But rehearsals all day and shows at night? My pediatrician, Dr. Bertram Roth, frowns when I say that I probably won't act again. He says a happy mother makes a happy baby, and I obviously won't be totally happy unless I act. He amazes me with this statement. How could he know me so well? Somehow, of course, it happens. Richard watches Sarah while he draws. During rehearsal breaks, I run down the Athenaeum stairs to the basement and out the back door and into our apartment to nurse her. I am playing Louka in Shaw's *Arms and the Man,* and a publicity photo of me with a low-cut peasant blouse, smoking a small cigar, takes up virtually one-third of the front page of the Sunday entertainment section. I think Corbin Patrick, Indianapolis News's theatre critic, likes zaftig women. The audiences seem to love Shaw here. They love his diatribes on war and prejudice. They love his women—so courageous and articulate. It's great to be back on the boards. The doctor is right.

Priscilla Lindsay

The Hummingbird Cafe

Once a week during the mid-seventies, I drove through the corn and soybean fields that stretched between my Crawfordsville home and the Hummingbird Cafe in Indianapolis. The cafe was at 22nd and Talbott Streets, in a neighborhood that was—and still is—a lively Bohemian artists' enclave amid vacant lots and derelict buildings. After I'd parked, I walked past dark warehouses and empty lots to get to the door. For me, the evening always began with this dose of urban, light-on-my-toes fugitive pride. A city dweller by birth, I was glad to escape the confines of small-town life.

Inside the Hummingbird was a lived-in warmth and grace. The aura of the sixties was still strong. Cappuccino, Double Mocha Latte—these had not been born yet, and no one noticed if the coffee was watery or the tea lukewarm. This was a place to read your poems and hear the work of others.

There was always a buzz about the small, crowded room. Who was there? How good were they? Who would get the response we all wanted—that hum when the audience sighs forward and seems to open to the rhythm or meaning of a line? Jeb Carter and Alice Friman, now "senior" Indianapolis poets and nationally known, practiced their poems at the Hummingbird in the seventies.

The small stage was grotto-like—lit, but with darkness filtering in from the edges of the room. The atmosphere wasn't in the decor—the indifferent lighting, the rickety tables with matchbooks tucked under their legs—but in the activity we brought, the passionate practice of saying words out across space and into the ears of others.

I made that long drive to the Hummingbird because Etheridge Knight was leading an ongoing workshop, teaching us how to say or read poems to an audience. I'm not sure these sessions had a name. Perhaps it was People's Poetry Workshop or Free People's Poetry. In other workshops I'd attended, people jockeyed for position, haggled over line breaks, or said things like "This poem would be better if. . . ." None of this happened at the Hummingbird. With his legendary generosity, Etheridge assumed the poems were good. We were there to practice and learn how to deliver them as living words to a live audience.

People often tell of Etheridge's extraordinary power as a reader. What I remember, particularly from those evenings, was his keen ability as a listener. When I approached the stage clutching my sheaf of poems, his advice was simple: "Take the space, stand behind your poem, speak out." He took great pride in saying his own poems, and we absorbed some of his natural dignity and resonance just by hearing him. Most often he spoke from memory. While I was reading, he might echo a line with one of his deep sighs of pleasure, of "yeah" or "yes, yes"—as in the Baptist call and response with which he'd grown up.

He was the most responsive audience I've ever had. Often, reading in front of an earnest college crowd, sitting silent with furrowed brows, I've wished he were still here. In those first years, Etheridge in the Hummingbird was the city to me—a human largeness, space, and freedom from small-town manners, a place to breathe.

Tam Lin Neville

Beltway

Not a hundred yards from the stretch of beltway I know best squats the subsidized complex where I lived for a decade. It is hemmed in by two other complexes—one with a fountain, one rammed up against a liquor store, all of them around a bend on Beachway from the ghost of the old cornflower-blue Westlake drive-in. Its gravel lot and speaker posts were replaced years ago by a flat black grade of asphalt, a Lowe's, a Blockbuster, a Cub Foods—warehouse shopping; buildings with ceilings so high that they have their own stratospheres. No more condoms or roach clips in the parking lots, no crack and fade to the speakers suspended among the dark metal beams.

Outside in those lots, however, an old droning remains in the air like burning ozone—the hum at five. You can hear the sizzle of wet tires and dull thump of a trunk-locked subwoofer losing itself in the Doppler of its arc onto the 10th Street ramp toward the Lindner's ice cream shop where I bought packs of sickening pink Bubble Yum.

We threw snowballs at semis from my junior high bus stop. We watched the swell and fury every May, and human beings—*people*—waving fanned clutches of race tickets from those boot-shaped, bomb-proof concrete dividers from Speedway to Deadman's Curve, which my high school friends and I navigated too fast during its construction. We took the curve at sixty-five, spilling burritos into our laps, counting the rubber streaks on the new concrete and talking of death, and then stepping on the gas and chirping the tires. People were living inches from the shatter and blur of flying metal, and were eating appetizers of burning gas and rubber just as they did at the "Track," waiting for something to happen.

Beyond the chain-link fence and sloped grass median marking the southern edge of Beachway Drive, the beltway is braided with ramps. There is no safe means by which to reach what is left of the neighborhood on the other side, behind the Sam's Club.

The people who take the ramps age and fix their hair in the rearview mirrors. As a school kid on cold winter mornings, I watched them live their lives with a ball of slush in my hand.

Sean Robisch

A Piece of the Hood

I grew up between a trailer park and the projects off 30th Street between Emerson and Arlington avenues. One night, a friend and I decided to meet another friend for dinner. About a half-hour before he was supposed to pick me up, he called.

"Ebony, I'm not going to make it out there tonight. My mother says that's not a very good neighborhood. It's already late, and I don't want to get lost."

I listened quietly. He was such a nice guy that he really didn't know that what he said was offensive. I told him it was okay and that we'd hook up another time, but we never did.

When I was growing up, I was never afraid to be out at night by myself. Home is the place where if I look out of my car window, I'll see other black people. If I'm lucky, they just might be singing along to the same song I'm singing along with, and when our eyes meet, we'll acknowledge our commonality. Home is the place where if it's above 60 degrees, there is always a basketball game. When it gets dark, they light up the driveway and keep on playing. Home is a neighborhood where the yards don't have grass, and if there is crabgrass, most of it is dead because people park their cars on it.

Home is poison ivy waiting if you go to the backyard to play; so the street is the spot. And there are countless children in the street jumping in front of cars on their way to school in the morning and again late at night. No one in the neighborhood seems to know the mothers of these children, but we all know their voices when they scream for their kids to come home.

Home is where young men squeal down the nearby highway on Japanese Ninja motor bikes at one o'clock in the morning. Home is a neighborhood with a church on every corner.

Now that I've grown up, and I come home as a visitor from college, I'm still not afraid; but I am more careful. Home is a neighborhood with its share of vacant houses, dimly lit streets, and liquor stores. Home is a place where the presence of police officers is increasing. Home is a place that city statistics and insurance policies classify as a high-risk area. My house is a place where my father just installed a motion-detecting floodlight on our six-by-four-foot front porch for "safety purposes."

Yet when I'm home, no one treats me differently. Sure, they're proud of me, but there's no pedestal for the girl who just might make it out of the ghetto. Instead, they support me as the young woman who's going out into the world to represent the good of our neighborhood. I'm proud not to be a product of the neighborhood's negativity, but a representative of its positive characteristics. And for those who misunderstand, who fear, or who just don't know, it's up to me to take a piece of the hood to them.

Ebony Utley

The Cradling Arm of **White River**

I live in a place called Ravenswood in the northeastern part of Indianapolis nestled in the cradling arm of the White River. I sometimes wish it were Raven's Wood, which somehow sounds a little more middle class. But it isn't middle class; it is really more of an indefinable class. Ravenswood preserves a unique kaleidoscope of people and wildlife. It is often overlooked and scorned by the affluent and the intellectual. The dead-end streets and cul-de-sacs discourage most outsiders from driving through more than once. The streets, so neglected that they resemble gravel roads more than city streets, soon convince drivers that slowness is more than a suggestion.

It is truly a woods, filled with squirrels, raccoons, opossums, muskrats, and beavers. I've seen osprey catch fish on the fly and blue heron, as still as statues, waiting in the marsh grass for a careless bass to swim by. Egrets flash their white plumage in homage to the sun as they wait patiently for their prey. Flicker, Downy, and Pileated Woodpeckers drum a rhythm of life on the bark of oak and maple and walnut and sycamore trees. Chickadees, titmice, and nuthatches liberally sprinkle the standard Indiana city bird population of cardinals, jays, sparrows, and starlings. An occasional oriole, goldfinch, and indigo bunting splash brilliant orange, yellow, and blue on my front yard feeder.

The people here are as unique as the animal species and the homes. There are towheaded children and junkyard dogs roaming the streets. Barefooted bicycle riders use vacant woods for motocross trails. Bare-chested boys jump in the river like Huck Finn, oblivious to the danger or the law. Fireworks reflect color on the waters of the White River every July 3rd, and gargantuan booms bounce from bank to bank. Beer drinkers strut from "Your Friendly Market" to the corner electronic games parlor.

Folks from the hills of southern Indiana, Kentucky, and West Virginia stop their beat-up, rusted out trucks in the middle of the street. With their driver's windows side by side and their vehicles facing opposite directions, they pepper the atmosphere with their hill accents until an impatient neighbor honks at them to move. Because the White River floods regularly, the houses are not too substantial. After a flood, people just wash out their houses, dig out the mud, put in new flooring, and go on. No one will ever mistake Ravenswood for a housing development. No house resembles another. Most started out as summer cottages and have been added onto one room at a time as the years and floods have gone by.

My immediate next-door neighbors are scavengers. They pick up discarded debris from here and there. They sort through it and sell anything they can. Then they put whatever's left out for the trash men.

Directly across the street, a man with a master's degree in business administration lives in an old camper trailer with no electricity or water. He drives a cement truck in the summers. He poured concrete all over his yard so that he can skate and drive go-carts on it. In the winter, he takes trips to Baja on his motorcycle or travels to Arkansas in his Porsche.

Next to him, a middle-aged hippie shares his home with a girlfriend, a fifteen-foot boa constrictor, and three very large rottweilers. He likes guns and trucks a lot.

Just east of him resides a family that has a dad who likes to drive go-carts and three-wheelers. These miniature muscle machines careen up and down our dead-end block every once in a while till someone threatens to call the police.

A few years ago, a man who lives to the west of us was shot by the jealous boyfriend of a woman he was dating. After he recovered, he cut down all the brush and some of the trees surrounding his house. Then he put up flood lights and a six-foot chain-link fence. And he bought a couple of chow dogs.

Several years ago, something happened that almost convinced me to move. A small group of drunk "good-ol'-boys" tried to burn a cross in the front yard of an African-American family that had just moved into the neighborhood. Fortunately, they were too dumb and too drunk to get it to burn. I talked with several of my neighbors after that. I found that we all had gone separately to visit the mother of the African-American family and told her one by one how sorry we were that this had happened. We said we hoped she'd stay. But that was scary, and I can understand why she decided to move. There are a couple of black families in the neighborhood now, and there's been no trouble this time.

I don't understand why I stay here sometimes. Then the snow falls and covers everything like a Currier and Ives print. Or I sit by the river and let the peace of God fill my battered city soul. Or I watch the birds on my feeder silhouetted by the brilliant green woods behind them, their bird songs echoing through the quiet of this small town in the middle of this booming city. And I know. I know.

Kate Webb

Out at the **Ballpark**

A number of people were of the opinion there was no rea-
son to leave Bush Stadium. They didn't see anything wrong with it. They'd come
out there for a game or two each year, and the grass was green and there was a
pretty brick wall with vines on it. I mean, what else is there? They didn't have to
live with it on a daily basis like we did, and know the problems with the wiring
and plumbing and superstructure of that stadium. And of course, Major League
Baseball had negotiated a deal with the minor leagues for so-called facilities
standards that were applied all across the country. Major League Baseball was
tired of having players that they'd recruited into professional baseball suddenly
playing in far worse facilities than they played in during college.

It had been a goal of mine to get a new baseball park for Indianapolis for
many years. I thought it needed to happen, even though I had the same nostal-
gic feelings the fans had for Bush Stadium. After all, I started watching games
there when I was just a boy. I was going to games in Bush Stadium from the time
I was a toddler back in the thirties and early forties. So I had that same feeling of
nostalgia. But on the other hand, as that park aged, I knew we were going to
have to have something new or we were going to lose baseball in Indianapolis.

When the new stadium opened, did I have a feeling of a dream come true? You get so caught up in the negotiations and the planning and the execution of the project that you don't have time for many other thoughts, I guess. All that's on your mind: When is it going to be ready? It would have been much easier for us to wait till the following April to open. But the mayor felt it needed to be completed, and he wanted to wrap it up. So we bit the bullet, moving from Bush to the new stadium at midseason, which was a logistical nightmare. Many of our people were working in a trailer out in the parking lot all through the rest of that season.

I'll tell you how tight things were. We had an open house for the public on July 9. We couldn't take people up to show them the suites and the press boxes, because the suites had just been finished and we were taking furniture and refrigerators up on the elevators all that day and all that evening—and the 10th and the early part of the 11th. That's how tight it was.

The wonderful thing was we had beautiful weather, not a hint of rain, and it was a very exhilarating ceremony that night before the game, with Mayor Goldsmith and Governor Bayh and Pat Early of the Capital Improvement Board, who really had a tremendous personal interest. Pat had been an usher for us in high school and his father Rex had been on the Indians board.

We had skydivers; Carl Erskine, the Dodgers' hall of famer who lives in Anderson, played the national anthem on the harmonica. Everything was wonderful—except we lost the game.

The major pressure was off after July 11. I really enjoyed the rest of the season. We had good weather. I think we had one rainout the rest of the season. We just really enjoyed the fact that the new stadium was being accepted so well by people in the community. We had huge crowds. And then you're able to sit there and think, "Well, we advertised that this was going to happen. And it happened."

Interview by Dan Carpenter

✻

Max Schumacher has been president of the Indianapolis Indians since 1961. On July 11, 1996, he realized a dream of replacing the beloved but decrepit Bush

Stadium on West 16th Street with a new, traditionally styled downtown ballpark. While the old ballpark had been named for the late Indians player and executive Owen Bush since 1967, many fans—Schumacher included—cherished the name it bore for twenty-five years beginning during World War II. Thus, Victory Field was reborn.

A Mere Two Minutes from Bustle

During hundreds of trips along College Avenue, I had no-
ticed cars parked just off the shoulder south of 75th Street. Sometimes, I'd catch
a glimpse of dogs bounding across the mowed field or of people sitting at wooden
picnic tables. But nothing compelled me to pull up, investigate, or even inquire
about the place. It looked like a typical roadside rest stop. I didn't know its name
because I hadn't bothered to read the words on the sign with the Indy Parks
logo. From my vantage point, either north- or south-bound at forty miles per
hour, it was there, but not.

Now, I parked beside a friend's waiting car.

"I can't believe you've never been here," said my friend, as she strode due
east across the field, her leashed dog straining toward what I now could see was
a wooded area.

Slipping between two trees, I felt like Alice down the rabbit hole. A mere
two minutes from bustle, I was in an old growth forest. Across the pathway, in a
north/south orientation, reclined an uprooted tree that must have reached at
least thirty feet skyward in its glory days. Even felled, it was imposing.

"This way to the river." My friend plunged forward, avoiding the right and left pathways at the juncture.

Ten minutes? Twelve? No matter. Time is marked by calls between birds. Single file, human conversation ceases. We had a destination. To the river. What more need be said? Now, this instant, all that mattered was marveling at the trees, lifting leafed branches, straight upward, claiming their portion of sunlight, absorbing the mix to keep on growing.

Then, with no warning, the denseness dissipated. Midday brilliant, blinding sunbeams bounced off the flood plain, skipped across a creek, and stopped at the impenetrable wall of forest lining the other bank.

"Wade across over here." My friend pointed to a spot downstream. "I think we can walk along the other side to get to where the creek empties into the White River."

The dog was already on her way. I stood stock-still.

How could I have been so inattentive as to pass up this amazing place? Here was a microcosm of what Indiana must have been like prior to becoming the nineteenth state. Mile after mile, hour after hour, was forest so dense that you felt encased or swaddled, depending on your frame of reference.

That moment offered a revelation and a rebuke. I'd shut out the availability of anything of indigenous value or interest off a main thoroughfare. I hadn't asked, "What's beyond that patch of grass?" Is it possible to discover a place that's already there?

Rita Kohn

why then
do we deal
treacherously?

A story is never just a story. It has the magic that makes us wonder at what we once took for granted. It has the power to change the status quo, to help us look at ourselves in new ways. If we can see things differently, perhaps we can make things different.

The customary way to consider a city in the heartland, a city like Indianapolis, is to see its homogeneity: The majority of its residents worship in familiar ways, come from similar backgrounds, eat the same foods, speak with distinctively regional accents. The gathering of immigrants may especially mark other urban centers, but not a Midwestern capital. Indianapolis is called the "Crossroads of America," and many people do travel through this city on their way to someplace else. It is not commonly viewed as an urban place where diversity takes up permanent residence. But maybe it appears this way because it is what we expect to see.

In the following pages are the stories of people who come from other places—Jerusalem, Bethlehem, Mexico, India, Pakistan, Afghanistan, Siberia, and Latvia—to make their homes in Indianapolis. To a city that is predominantly Protestant and Roman Catholic, they bring the practice of many faiths: Judaism, Greek Orthodoxy, Sikhism, and Islam. You also find stories of people who are native born but who have been made to feel like outsiders because of their race.

A city is defined by how it treats the "stranger," the one who is different. The quality of urban life is characterized not by how we live out our individual lives, going about our own business, but by how we relate to one another, to the other who is unlike us. A city is measured by how we make connections and create a society that both celebrates diversity and builds unity.

To maintain a sense of the holy in the everyday, religion helps make the commonplace extraordinary. It helps us see the mystery, the wonder in the mundane. Building community, forging a sense of shared purpose, requires us to make the strange familiar, to understand what we hold in common. The following narratives invite us to see ourselves in the other and the other in ourselves.

Have we not all one Father,
has not one God created us?
Why then do we deal treacherously
one against the other?

—Malachi 2:10

Inside the Melting Pot

It's the summer of 1950. Mrs. Čigāns is an expert on America; she has been here for three months. She unerringly picks out the newly arriving Displaced Persons at the Indianapolis train station.

Her name means Gypsy, but she looks American. She strides ahead boldly, her clothes like nothing we have seen. She is wearing a dress of some strange aqua material, neither cotton nor linen, with a circle-cut full skirt. Her waist is nipped in by a wide black belt that seems to be made out of rubber, her black hair is pinned up in hornlike rolls away from her face. Her legs are shapely and strong, and black hairs curl provocatively over the white bobby socks thrust into high-heeled black patent-leather shoes. She stops waving the scarf she has been using to attract our attention and expertly knots it so that two rabbit ears nod above her forehead. She takes out a compact and checks her bright red lipstick.

"Now, girls," she says as soon as we are settled in a taxi, "you will have to watch out, this isn't safe little Germany, oh no." She laughs and inspects her glistening red nails. "Oh no, not at all. See that light? You have to move fast when it's green and never start to cross the street when it's yellow, don't even *think* about it."

A siren sounds in the distance, very faint but growing louder, more familiar, more ominous.

"Yes," she says. "When you hear that, run as fast as you can and jump on the sidewalk. If you are scared, stay close to the buildings and away from the street until you get used to it. But always hop on the sidewalk as quick as you can; otherwise, the police will drive right over you, they'll flatten you like you were made of wet clay, they won't stop to take you to the hospital or cemetery. Things move fast here in America, so you have to hurry up."

The ambulance screeches by the halted taxi. "See what I mean?"

My sister and I put our heads together and whisper.

"And another thing," Mrs. Čigāns says, "Don't think you can talk to each other in Latvian, you can't. They don't like it, the Americans. You always have to speak English. You are inside the melting pot," she adds mysteriously.

Sometime later, Mrs. Čigāns takes me to the Indianapolis Public Library, an imposing gray building that spans an entire block. Our steps echo over the marble floors, through the cavernous rooms and long galleries.

She conducts the negotiations with the elderly blue-haired librarian who looks at me suspiciously. Finally, the librarian sighs elaborately and starts typing. She pecks out a few letters, sighs again, types some more, and hands me a yellow card.

Alcoves, balconies, dim rooms—all are full of books, one ceiling-high bookcase after another, rows and rows of them. I have never seen so many books in one place; I have held very few books that are not flimsily bound and printed on cheap yellow paper that crumbles easily. I will read these one by one, I will try to read them all, and I will learn everything I need to know. If I read three every week, how long will it take to get through them all? I cannot wait to begin. But first I have to learn English. Is that possible?

Mrs. Čigāns confers with the librarian again. "Whoosh, whoosh," she says and waves her arms. The librarian stares at her. Mrs. Čigāns cups her hands around her mouth and blows. "Oh," says the librarian and clicks away over the white marble floor. She returns with *Gone With the Wind*.

Mrs. Čigāns translates. I feel a smile of pure joy breaking out on my face, so that the librarian remembers why she became a librarian in the first place and smiles too. She stamps the book and hands it directly to me. My mouth is dry, and my hands tremble; I can't wait to get home.

Gone With the Wind has been translated into Latvian and published in the Displaced Persons' camps in four separate small paperback volumes. My mother owns only the first volume, which I have read three times already. Will Scarlett O'Hara get Ashley Wilkes to fall in love with her and marry her? Will she fall in love with Rhett Butler instead? Will she have to leave Tara? What will happen to her during the war? Will she survive? Will she ever be able to return to her home? I burn to know.

As soon as I get back to the Pastor's house, I find the English/Latvian dictionary that my parents, nonsmokers both, have gotten by saving and trading their cigarette allocations. At the head of the stairs going up to the attic is a door that opens onto a tiny balcony that no one ever uses. The railing is wobbly, and the space is so small that it is suitable only for one person. It is a perfect place—light, silent, and shady most of the day. No one ever sits there.

I begin by comparing words in the Latvian translation with words on the first page of English. I search the dictionary for those I do now know. Some of them appear with puzzling variations and approximations; others are not listed at all. But most are. Line by line, painstakingly, I work through sentences, then paragraphs of the material already so familiar in Latvian. When a word or sentence refuses to yield, I go to another, worried that I will always understand just parts. But I continue.

Hours later the book falls open in the middle. "I'm never going to be hungry again," Scarlett promises herself. This is not a part I have read before in Latvian. I look up each word, and then, keeping my fingers in different parts of the dictionary, I stare at the whole sentence. A miraculous intense knowledge, like light, fills me. I understand this. I understand. "I'm never going to be hungry again." I realize I will be able to figure out the unknown parts of the book; I will teach myself English. I am elated. The sun setting over the maple tree in the backyard seems to confirm it.

Agate Nesaule

✼

An earlier version of this essay appeared in A Woman in Amber: Healing the Trauma of War and Exile *(Soho Press, 1995).*

No One Else Did Anything

My high school was one of the places where I assumed I was safe. However, it was in this presumably safe place—a prestigious private high school—that I learned about prejudice in my junior year. Every year, the school gave an award for the top history paper written by a junior student. My history instructor was engaging. He caused the students to dig deep and never accept anything on the surface. I felt energized in his class.

The day came when the essay award was announced. I was the winner. One of my classmates who had not distinguished himself as a top student was so upset that his paper had not been chosen that he came over to my desk and demanded to see my paper. He called me a "dumb nigger" in front of the whole class. I asked the teacher, "Aren't you going to do something about this?" He said, "No."

I immediately went to see the headmaster and told him what had occurred. He asked, "What should I do about it?"

I said, "The student should apologize to me, and so should the teacher."

The headmaster left me sitting in his office for awhile. When he returned he advised me, "I think that we should just forget this happened. We have to consider the student who made the remark. His father works for a prominent company; his family is wealthy. You are a scholarship student. It is best to over-look his obvious ignorance."

I was sixteen years old and appalled that nothing was going to be done. I found this response hard to accept. I called my mother from school to ask for her advice. She told me to go back to class and to finish the school day. We agreed to discuss the matter when I got home. That evening, my parents and I talked. This was not the first time that we had to deal with this type of issue. When the school choir performed at places with racially discriminatory policies, I did not want to participate. My parents discussed this issue with the music teacher, and I was excused from those performances.

This time, my father said that he was going to leave the response to this incident up to me. My parents pledged to stand behind me no matter what I decided. "Remember," my father cautioned, "You are a scholarship student. You may need to be prepared to make other arrangements for your schooling." I was prepared.

By now everyone at school knew about the incident. I told the headmaster that I thought the student who made the racial slur should apologize to me during morning assembly and explain to the student body why racial slurs are both inappropriate and unacceptable. The headmaster rejected my request. Instead, the headmaster appealed to a member of the school's board of directors. The person approached was the father of another African-American student in my class. In the past, I stood up for this man's son. Some of the boys called my classmate "Kunta Kinte," hero of the movie "Roots," which had just been re-leased. I said, "You shouldn't call him that name. It is not his name." Afterward, the boys stopped calling him Kunta Kinte, except in front of me. Now the father of my classmate was asked to convince me to withdraw my complaint, because, after all, he would not want the incident to jeopardize his own son.

In the end, nothing happened. One girl in the class told me she had dis-cussed my experience with her parents and that her parents thought what had occurred was inappropriate. This student was the only person in a class of more than fifty students who ever talked to me about what happened. No one else did anything.

I received the history award without incident and graduated from the school the next year. I learned that prejudice and racism exist at every level. I was in a school and community with a group of well-educated and enlightened people. I realized that I was not safe from intolerance anywhere.

Twenty years later, I saw the student who made the racial slur. My husband recently passed away as a result of severe injuries sustained in a terrible automobile accident caused by two drivers who were drunk and drag racing. We had been married only five months. When my former classmate heard about my husband's death, he called me. I never received an apology, but during this difficult time in my life, my classmate really became a friend.

Interview by Sandy Eisenberg Sasso

❦

Marya Jones Overby came to Indianapolis with her family when she started first grade in 1966. She is a graduate of Harvard University and Indiana University School of Law. She is Of Counsel at Sommer & Barnard in Indianapolis.

Only Once a Year

My daughter Phyllis loved to read. When she was three, she tried to read her books. She would point and ask, "What's that?" attempting to pronounce the name of the person or thing. One day, she realized the people in the book didn't look like any people she had seen. There was a white man pictured in the book as a farmer. Phyllis had never seen a white farmer—or any other farmer. She seemed puzzled by it.

Shortly after trying to explain about the white farmer, an agent from Metropolitan Life Insurance Company came to our house to discuss our insurance policy. He would also collect for it each week. When the agent came to the door, Phyllis ran to the door shouting, "Farmer, farmer!" I suppose she thought that if he's a white man, he must be a farmer. "No," I said; "this is the insurance man; his name is Mr. Quiggels."

Phyllis broke out in gales of laughter; she was holding her little stomach and rolling on the floor. "Quiggels?" she said, "Quiggels?" She couldn't stop laughing. I was so embarrassed, but Mr. Quiggels began to laugh too.

He was completely enchanted by this three-year-old cut-up. They became friends, and he called her Sweet Pea. Every Monday, when Mr. Quiggels came to collect for the insurance, Phyllis was waiting with her book. They would sit on the steps in the summer, and he would read to her, until years later, when she read to him. He was loving and patient. They had a friendship that I sometimes envied. To her, there was no one like Quiggels. As soon as he stepped to the door and said, "Where's my Sweet Pea," she would run and grab his hand and say, "Hi, Quiggels; let's read a story!" This continued for many years.

When Phyllis was old enough, I took her to Riverside Amusement Park on Milk Top Day. We went once a year till Phyllis was eight. The children couldn't wait till milk top day at Riverside Park. Admission was based on the number of tops you saved from Polk milk bottles. We boarded the bus, along with friends and relatives, anticipating a fun-filled day at the park. A few hours after arriving at the park, I noticed Phyllis had the inquisitive look that I dread on her face. "What's wrong?" I asked.

"Why don't we come to the park every week? It would be fun to come every week," she moaned.

I didn't know how to tell her, but I knew I had to tell her the truth. I hesitated for a moment. She was waiting for an answer, and her expression seemed to say, I don't think I'm going to like your answer. I cleared my throat. "We can only come once a year," I said with a lump in my throat.

"Why?"

"Because colored people are not allowed to come more often than one day a year."

"Who won't let us come?"

"The people who own the park," I answered, hoping that would end the questions.

She was quiet for a moment, then she asked, "Are we colored people?"

"Yes."

"Are the people that own the park white people?"

"Yes," I said, hoping that this was the last question. I could see she was still thinking and not satisfied with my answer.

"Why don't they want us to come?"

She was relentless, and I wasn't prepared; but I knew I had to answer her. "Honey, there are, unfortunately, some white people who don't like colored people; and because they own the park, they can decide who comes to the park and when."

I knew I had handled it badly, but I was sure that settled it for now. I would discuss it later, when I thought she would understand.

Phyllis looked up at me, with her eyes narrowed and her jaw set. "They don't know me, so how can they not like me? I will never come back to this park again. I'm going to talk to Quiggels about this!"

With that announcement, she stomped off to catch up with her friends. I reproached myself for not handling it better. I was never quite prepared for some of Phyllis' questions, but I would never discourage her from asking. She was quiet all the way home and talked very little over the weekend.

On Monday, Phyllis was sitting on the steps, waiting for her friend Quiggels. When he saw her, he said, "Hey, Sweet Pea, are we going to read a story?"

"No," she snapped and got up and went into the house.

Mr. Quiggels was taken aback; he had never seen her unhappy and sullen before. "What's the matter with Sweet Pea?" he asked.

"Just growing up a little," I said, not knowing how to answer him.

Mr. Quiggels recorded my insurance payment and went out and sat at his usual place on the steps. Shortly, Phyllis came out and sat down beside him. From the sofa in the living room, I couldn't hear all that Phyllis said, but I did hear just enough to know she was talking to him about Riverside Park. I heard her very clearly when she said, "Quiggels, are we friends?"

"Of course," he answered enthusiastically.

"Do you like me even though I'm colored?" she asked in a voice that almost broke my heart.

Mr. Quiggels responded, "No, I don't only like you, I love you because you're my Sweet Pea; and if I owned that park, I would let you come anytime you wanted to."

She laid her head against his shoulder, and they sat silently for a while. Finally, Phyllis got up and came into the house. She didn't tell Mr. Quiggels goodbye. As she passed, I could see her feathery eyelashes glistening from the tears she had not allowed to fall.

When Mr. Quiggels got up from the steps, his face was red and his voice was hoarse as he said, "I'll see you next week, Mrs. Adair." He shouted a goodbye to Phyllis. "Bye, Sweet Pea," but she didn't answer.

Before he got to the end of the walk and through the gate, Phyllis ran past me, almost stepping on my feet, on past the porch, and stopped halfway between the porch and the gate. She yelled, "Quiggels, will you always be my friend?"

"Always and forever, Sweet Pea, always and forever. I promise," he assured her.

She ran and jumped into his arms and said, "Then, I will always be your friend."

In the years that followed, Quiggels kept his promise, and so did she.

Interview by Phyllis J. Adair

This story is written in the voice of my mother, Prudence Knox Adair. Prudence is the fifth of twelve children and was born July 8, 1909, in Homer, Georgia, in Banks County. The family moved to Indianapolis in 1919 to escape threats from the Ku Klux Klan. Their first home was in Brightwood on Station Street, on the east side of Indianapolis. At eighty-nine years old, Prudence still enjoys telling stories about her life.

A Turban in the **City-County Building**

I left my home in India with my family in September 1947. I was seven years old. Our family lost everything in the partition of India. It was genocide. Tens of thousand of people were murdered. My family was dumped on the sidewalk. It was a time of great terror, and we had several encounters with death. People were fleeing for their lives. Sometimes, trains were stopped at the border, and the passengers were slaughtered. I was witness to all that. That is my story, my soul.

I came to America in 1965 and to Indianapolis in September 1967. I had just completed a second master's in city planning. I was quite impressed that the city hadn't made the kind of progress that some other major cities were making. The city had only one way to go. I thought that I could be part of a group to change the vision of the city from India-no-place to "India-some-place."

The very first evening newspaper, the *Indianapolis News,* had a very small heading under the title, "Did you see . . . ?" When I arrived they wrote, "Did you see a turban and a bearded man looking like an Indian maharajah viewing the children's exhibit in the lobby of the City-County Building?"

You can see how novel, how unusual it was to have a Sikh in the heart of the city, in the downtown, in the City-County Building. That was for me a signal that there was some work to be done here to educate people about who I was. If you forget the turban and the beard part of it, I just breathe the same air and laugh the same way. There is a heart that beats inside and a mind that wanders at a thousand miles an hour. Besides my architectural planning, I felt that I needed to commit myself to be an educator as to my background, my faith, my culture, my country. I have never stopped since that time serving on committees and in many different ways.

Over the course of several days in 1967, I encountered reluctance on the part of an apartment complex to rent an apartment to me. Although the sign said that apartments were available, the owners saw me and my unusual dress. They decided that no, the apartment was filled. It was taken up that morning.

There was another situation when I went into a bar. I was told that in this bar, you must take your hat off to be served a drink. And I said "This turban is not a hat, this is part of my religious dress and I do not take it off in public. I am a Sikh."

The bartender said, "Well, in that case, you cannot be served a drink in this bar."

I decided not to make anything out of it. I was with some friends, and we stepped away.

Over the months that followed, there were questions. People asked, "If you are to become a U.S. citizen, are you still planning to keep your turban and beard?" I had to explain to them at each place that my appearance has nothing to do with my being a citizen. I am committed to this country. The turban and beard are part of my faith, and that is a private, personal commitment between me and my God.

There were other jokes and questions that came from time to time. My children were born at Methodist Hospital. I was asked, "Were your children born with a turban already on?"

But some of it was all kidding between friends. Yet you could see a certain lack of sensitivity, a certain amount of ignorance at some places, a certain amount of rudeness at other places. But that is all behind us.

A moment stands tall in my memory. In the fall of 1995 at the Ambassadors' Ball, I was called to the podium of the Indiana Roof to receive the Sagamore of the Wabash. Everyone knew I was going to receive the award, but I did not. Everything in the past has been transcended by the future. My dress no longer matters. That night I wore a tuxedo and my maroon turban.

Interview by Sandy Eisenberg Sasso

K. P. Singh was born in India, came to the United States in 1965, and has made Indianapolis his home since 1967. His distinctive pen and ink drawings of historic architecture and monuments from Indiana and around the world combine the skills of an architect, artist, and historian. Singh was the founding director of the International Center. There are two hundred Sikh families in Indianapolis who get together for worship at the Sikh Temple on the southeast side of the city.

We Prayed to **One God**

I was born in India and lived with my parents there for eighteen years. When they migrated to Pakistan, I went to Karachi to study medicine. In 1969, I came to the United States to study medicine in Chicago and, three years later, moved to Indianapolis to complete my training at Indiana University. I never thought much about interfaith issues; I was more concerned about my medical studies. I knew little about people of other faiths, hardly ever meeting them in my own country.

When I first came to Indianapolis, it was not easy to be a Muslim in a collective way. I could pray by myself, fast by myself, and give charity by myself, but there were few people with whom to visit and socialize, and food was a major problem. I always worried whether I would be served alcohol or pork or something made with lard. There was a lot of ignorance about Islam in the media. Muslims were often labeled as terrorists. One of my patients used to fight with his co-workers, saying that Muslims are not terrorists. "Look at my doctor," he'd say. "He's kind and caring. How can he be a terrorist?"

I joined the Interfaith Alliance in Indianapolis. It was one of the best things that happened in my life. For the first time, I saw members of other faiths as children of God. They learned about Muslims, and I learned about Christians, Jews, Buddhists, Hindus, Baha'i, and Sikhs. One evening, a rabbi and I were invited to a minister's house for dinner. When the time came for my sunset prayer, I excused myself to go into a different room to pray. The reverend asked me if I would pray in the same room and if he and the rabbi could join me in prayer. I offered the formal Islamic prayer, and the reverend and the rabbi prayed behind me. Then together we offered a personal prayer. We realized that we did pray to one God.

One of my sweetest memories was in the month of Ramadan, a month of fasting in the Muslim tradition. I was surprised to receive a gift of delicious dates from Palm Springs. They were sent by my Jewish friend for our family to break the fast.

But there were times that were not as pleasant. During the Gulf War, there was much hostility against Muslims. Muslims were being identified with Saddam Hussein. My son, a high school student, was taunted as an Iraqi though he had never been to Iraq. My wife was called an Iranian because of the head cover she wore. During that frightening time, a priest called me and said, "Shahid, I am worried about you. What can I do for your safety?" I said, "Father Tom, all security is from God, but you can do something for my community."

Father Tom spoke publicly and issued a statement in the newspaper saying that Muslims in Indianapolis have nothing to do with what was happening in the Middle East. Their lives and honor should be respected as would the lives and honor of other Americans.

Love is a two-way street, so when I heard about missiles falling on Israel, I called my rabbi friend to give sympathy to the Jewish people. He publicly thanked me in a congregational prayer.

I have never been to Iran, but if I do go, I can tell them that "America is not the great Satan." I have four children born and raised here in Indianapolis. They and my wife are thankful to God to have given us Indianapolis as our home on this planet.

Interview by Sandy Eisenberg Sasso

❀

Dr. Shahid Athar is a practicing physician, writer, and speaker on Islam. He is the author of numerous books on Islam, including Reflections of an American Muslim.

Best to Work with Your Hands

My family came to East Chicago from Mexico in 1957. I was eleven years old. I came from a warm Mexican climate, and we moved there in the middle of December. I felt like a summer plant uprooted.

Ten years later, my father left and I became the head of the household that included my mother, four sisters, and two brothers. I was twenty-one years old, and my youngest sister was one. I became the breadwinner. I wanted to get my brothers and sisters to college, so when a position opened up at the State Capital in Indianapolis, I applied and was accepted.

I left my family in East Chicago and rented an apartment at 38th Street. I felt lost. I would get on I-65 and not know where to exit. I drove home every weekend. It was tough, but I knew my goal was to bring my whole family to Indianapolis. I did that in 1981.

Most of all, I wanted an education. When I went to high school in East Chicago, my school counselor told me, "You know, Maria, you Mexicans are best to work with your hands." That motivated me to get an education, to prove her wrong. About the time I came to Indianapolis, a young girl of Mexican-American descent who was attending Indiana University–Purdue University

Indianapolis (IUPUI) was killed in a traffic accident. Her mother took all of her daughter's savings and gave them to the financial aid office of IUPUI to establish a scholarship for Hispanic students. With that money, I was able to start college.

I was the first Hispanic to serve in the Governor's office. I worked in Human Resources for Governor Bowen. The secretary of the executive assistant welcomed me into her home. My teachers at IUPUI reached out to me. They were a blessing.

I learned to survive because of my faith. I believe that I am a creation of God, created in God's image, and if people have a problem with my heritage, sex, or color, well, that's not my problem. When I have a bad experience, I block it from my mind. I focus on the positive.

I always felt welcome in Indianapolis. When my siblings, who were born in Indiana, are asked where they are from because of their Spanish last name, they get annoyed. They say, "We're Hoosiers. We're from Indiana!"

Interview by Sandy Eisenberg Sasso

❀

Maria Tapia emigrated from Mexico in 1957 when she was eleven years old. She came to Indianapolis in 1973. She worked in the Indiana Civil Rights Commission from 1978–81 and is presently a television and radio producer and director.

The Only White Left

Mr. Lyons is now the oldest resident on the block of 34th and Graceland. His house is still huge, white trimmed in black, and although he lives alone, there's always someone visiting. He still cuts through the alley just like everybody did back then, and he says it's too bad I can't see the cherry and peach trees that were once in his backyard so I could understand why he never used the front very much.

Back in the fifties, you could boast about being the first or second black person on the block, as Mr. Lyons did. But then there was also the embittered German neighbor across the street who let it be known she wouldn't stand for his dump truck being parked in front of her house so she could not see what the "niggers" were up to. I know Mr. Lyons took it in stride and recognized that for all of the malcontents fighting hard against the winds of change, there were others like the Robards next door who made up for this hostility well into the next generation.

Mrs. Robards was the one who said that, try as she might, she couldn't prepare those cherries and peaches for the kids on the block without making them sick. While the other whites were moving out, they pitied folks like Mrs.

Robards who could only afford to die off around us blacks who were increasing in number.

Who knows if that was on Mrs. Robards' mind? Back then, she seemed to be more concerned with her efforts to turn sour, indigestible fruit into pies that her neighbors' youngsters could enjoy. After too many of her failed attempts and too many sick children who slithered into Mr. Lyons' back yard to sample directly from his trees (only to leave with loose bowels), Mr. Lyons acted on her suggestion to cut down the trees. That seemed to be the only way to prevent curious neighborhood children from sneaking the forbidden fruit.

Running wild with my playmates in a frenzied chorus and jumping free of the bushes that hugged the front of our house, my friends and I were warned to mind our manners and not impose our intoxication on Mrs. Robards. Maybe such consideration was extended because she was childless. And by the time we were born, she was widowed and living alone. But as a youngster, I saw this as even more promising because there was little to compete with the attention I received from her.

Graceland Avenue would not have been the same without being able to run next door and climb onto Mrs. Robards' porch swing when no one was looking or go inside her sweet-smelling house and find something to interest both young and old, black and white. As I grew older, I would go to greet her at the bus stop on the corner after she descended from the 27th and Butler bus. By this time in the early to mid-eighties, she was the only white person left, but this fact didn't register until much later. As long as Mrs. Robards lived next door, I never thought about racism or ethnic identity as something to be struggled with.

Maybe that is why—after she was put into a nursing home shortly before her death—I would return to that swing on the porch of her vacant house out of respect for the life that once was there. I had to sort it all out then. Although Mrs. Robards was gone, I knew she had never abandoned the neighborhood.

Khemli Ezell

My Business **Doubled**

My home was in Kabul, Afghanistan. It was beautiful. We had a three-story house, land, and gardens. Our women were educated; they were doctors. Now, on television I see only mountains and desert. Now, since the Taliban came to power, a woman can leave her house only when escorted by a man.

I left Kabul when I was nineteen to study civil engineering in Kiev. When the situation worsened in my country, I left Russia to come to Bloomington, Indiana, because my sister and brother-in-law were students at Indiana University. I didn't want anyone in Russia to know that I was planning to settle in the United States, so I left everything in my Kiev dormitory. I came with nothing—not even a picture of my home.

When the Russians invaded Afghanistan, my father was jailed by the Communists for two years as a political prisoner. When he was released, he needed medical attention. His kidneys were failing because of the torture he endured in prison. I moved to Indianapolis from Bloomington so that I could bring my father to St. Vincent's hospital for dialysis. For two years, I didn't work; I took care of my parents. After a time, I opened an Afghani restaurant, Kabul, on the north side of the city, and I have never left.

I have helped to bring other family members to Indianapolis. Last Thanksgiving, we could no longer fit into my house for dinner. We were more than sixty people—brothers, sisters, uncles, and their families. I had to open the restaurant so we could all have a place to sit. We didn't eat Afghan food; we ate turkey.

When I was working as a bus boy in a Bloomington restaurant, I saw a customer walking to the kitchen door. I asked if I could help him. He said he was looking for John. I knew there was a waiter named John, and I brought him over to the customer. I said, "Here is John." The customer told me he was looking for the toilet.

Now I am a Hoosier. My three children were born here. I am not certain that I will return to Kabul. I left there after high school. This is my home, and I feel welcomed here. Of course, as long as you have an accent and look different, people still consider you a foreigner. The only difference is that their families just came a few years earlier than I did. But I am treated well, and I have never felt any prejudice. I belong to the Jewish Community Center. Now, here I am a Muslim, but when I go there, I feel like I belong. It is a part of me. I have more Jewish friends than people of any other religion.

Once when I was driving my father in the city, we passed by a church, and he asked me to stop so we could pray there. I said, "Dad, we are Muslim, and that is a church." But my father said that we can pray to God anywhere—in a church, a synagogue, a mosque, or at home." He taught me that what matters is being a good citizen, a good person.

I have people working at the restaurant from all different countries—from France, Russia, New Zealand, the Czech Republic. I tell my Afghan relatives that I do not look at where people are from. I look for people who will do the right job.

After the terrorist attack of September 11, 2001, something amazing happened. The restaurant was more crowded than ever. My business doubled. People were coming to support me. When I was too busy cooking in the kitchen, my customers left notes for me. They said, "God bless you. We are glad that you are doing fine. We support you." My customers are more than clients. They are my friends.

Interview by Sandy Eisenberg Sasso

❁

Nasir Ayoubi has lived in Indiana for twenty-seven years. He is the owner of Kabul restaurant on the north side of the city.

If You Stop, **You Drown**

The first time I ran into racism was in my own home. I lived on the 3500 block of Central Avenue in a brick house. My mother would entertain on the patio toward the front of the house. I will never forget a friend I played with at the church near my home, Tabernacle Presbyterian. He was black. His father took care of the church. The church wasn't integrated. I don't think there was an integrated church at that time, in the early thirties. One day, my friend and I rode our bikes all the way from the church up the driveway of my house. My mother was entertaining. She was upset because I had brought a black child to the house while she had guests. I had never seen anybody upset about this before. I was seven years old. It made me aware that people were treated differently, but I didn't buy it. I just knew that it was wrong, unfair to judge somebody by skin color.

After my teenage years, I came to the conclusion that there was a Truth. You might get there through the synagogue, the church, or Plato. There are lots of ways of getting there. I knew that racism didn't make sense intellectually; it was an issue of fairness. Religion had much to do with it.

There has been tremendous progress since that time—for some, but not for all. There is a sea of prejudice. You can swim through it, but if you stop, you drown.

In the sixties when we were organizing for the Urban League, I was going to have lunch with Henry J. Richardson, Jr., the first black member of the Indianapolis legislature in the twentieth century. He invited me to come to the Columbia Club. We went to the dining room to sit down. The headwaiter, who was black, said that Mr. Richardson could not eat in the dining room. I said, "What?" I didn't know that. Henry knew, but he had wanted me to find out by myself. I was embarrassed, of course. We got up and left. I apologized, "I'm sorry; I had no idea."

We decided to go down to the Athletic Club. We didn't know whether we could get seated there, but we went in. A black headwaiter greeted us there also. He asked, "Well, Mr. Binford, Mr. Richardson, where can I seat you?" I said, "Thank God." We thought we would be turned down, but we weren't turned down. I think that decision was made by the headwaiter at that time. I found out later that they did permit blacks in the private dining room, but they had not in the public areas. This might have been the first time a black person was permitted into the public dining area.

As an adult, I had not actually experienced racism personally before this incident. I knew there were places where blacks couldn't go, but I had never tested it or done anything about it. This was all coming as a shock to this little white boy who lived in a white neighborhood and went to a private white school. Not even in the army during World War II did I come face to face with racism because there was no integration among the troops.

When I was Chairman of the Indiana Civil Liberties Union, I remember one of my customers stopped buying from me. I received an anonymous letter in which the author threatened to catch me in the alley with a rusty knife.

Henry Richardson didn't encourage me to get out in front. He said, "You run with the dogs and the foxes." I could talk to the blacks and the whites. I give him credit for training me.

When the issue of school integration arose in the late sixties, the Executive Committee of the Chamber of Commerce agreed to a position on integration of the schools. One of the brightest leaders on the committee said, "We don't have

to announce this position. We'll put it in a safe and if we need it, we'll use it."
They really didn't favor the policy then. So they were a bunch of hypocrites.

I think that things have changed. Blacks and whites have a good relationship, but people like myself can get fooled. Still, I believe we are better than
people think we are. If you give Hoosiers a problem, and they know the story of
unfairness, the poverty, the need, they react well. Their hearts and values are
good, but ignorance and prejudice can get in the way.

Interview by Sandy Eisenberg Sasso

❊

*Tom Binford (1924–99) was involved in business, civic, and sporting endeavors
in Indianapolis for more than fifty years. He played a critical role in the city's
desegregation efforts as a member of the Greater Indianapolis Progress Committee (GIPC). He also founded the Urban League of Indianapolis in 1965 and
was chairman of the Indiana state committee of the U.S. Civil Rights Commission
from 1972 to 1976. Binford was also the chief steward of the Indianapolis 500
from 1974 to 1995.*

We Started from Nothing

When I was growing up, I never thought about living in the United States. I had a scholarship to go to college at any Arab university in 1978–79. I went to the University of Bethlehem, but I didn't finish. The first years, there were always strikes and demonstrations. The school would open for a week and then close for a month. I got a visa to come the United States in December 1979 to get an education.

When I left, I was really mad. I had been put in prison in Israel for no reason and was kept there for three weeks. My parents didn't know where I was. Then I was let go. There were no charges against me. When this happened and I had a chance to go to the United States, I went.

I left my home in Bethlehem for Indianapolis on January 7, 1980. I am Greek Orthodox, and it was Christmas day for me. On January 8, my first day in the city, there was a big snowstorm. I had never seen snow. I thought, how am I going to live here? The first six months were hard. I wanted to go back home.

Day by day, things got easier. My parents arrived eight months after I did, in August 1980, and then two other brothers came as well. Your family helps you get by.

We decided to buy a restaurant in 1982. We took it as a joke. It was something to keep my parents busy, and it would provide extra cash. My mom always cooked, and she raised six kids. This was something she knew how to do.

It was very hard at the beginning. We started from nothing. We had nobody. We had to do it ourselves. Social life is different here. People are always busy. But with determination, we took all the steps. My house, my marriage, my kids—this is the home that I have built. In the last five years, things have been going well. People get to know you, trust you. They know that you care about them. For me, business is second; people are first. We take care of people.

The people who come to eat here at the restaurant are from the neighborhood, from Butler University and Clowes Hall, the Children's and Art Museum. There are Christian Theological Seminary professors. I have seen kids growing up, so many divorces and remarriages. People die. One man had a heart attack at the restaurant. He is gone, but his wife still comes here. She always sits in the same front booth. Some of the kids of customers start working here. I hear sad stories and good stories. I hardly have to write down my customers' food orders. I know them all.

It is very nice to live here compared with other cities. It's quiet, and in our restaurant, there is a good chance to be in touch with other people in Indianapolis. It helps us to get to know Indianapolis from the people. I have seen life in other cities—Detroit, Chicago. Indiana is better. Try to drive in Washington, D.C. Indianapolis is great. When I'm in these other places, I cannot wait to get home. For me, Indianapolis is the best town.

The landlord of my restaurant is Jewish. Seventy-five percent of my customers are Jewish. We don't have anything against each other. I wish we could get along in Israel like we do here. We want to see peace in the Middle East; we pray for it.

Sometimes, there is prejudice. During the Gulf War, some people threatened to bomb our place. They left notes in the door of the restaurant. But except for some teenage pranks, there is no real crime here. The street is nice and quiet.

I have lived half of my life here, and I feel that this is my home, but you never forget the place where you come from. I still have family there—brothers, sisters, cousins, my wife's family. I married in July 1992. My wife is from Bethlehem. I wanted to marry someone from the old country with the same religion, the same values. We still return to Bethlehem to visit. My birthplace is the place where Jesus was born.

When we are here, we call home every week. We find out who is getting married or divorced, who is having children, who has died. We stay in touch by reading our home newspapers on the Internet. We are happy living here, but we know what happens there.

I want my kids to grow up in Indianapolis. I have a good business, a good neighborhood. My church has 400–500 members. It was started by my ancestors from Lebanon and Syria, Jordan and Palestine in the early twentieth century. I am very connected to the church. The service is mostly in English, but there is some Arabic. When we baptized our daughter, the priest tried to do it in Arabic. I want my children to know their native language. We speak Arabic at home.

The United States is international for everybody. There are no real Americans except for the Indians. We are all foreigners. Sometimes, because of my English dialect, people know I am not from here. But I feel like I'm living at home, paying taxes and trying to live my life in peace.

Interview by Sandy Eisenberg Sasso

❧

Nihad Bannourah was born in Bethlehem. He came to Indianapolis in 1980 and attended Indiana University–Purdue University Indianapolis. He received a degree in business with a major in accounting. He is the owner of Banura's, a popular Middle Eastern restaurant on the north side of the city that was reopened in spring 2002.

No One Shouts, No One Interrupts

My path has been a long one, from Israel to Europe to Hong Kong to California to my new home in Indianapolis. It feels especially cold and dark, and I'm gloomy and lonely. I'm away from family, and I miss the smells, the music, and the Hebrew books of my birthplace. But on this Sunday in December, I find a way to pursue the same passion that drove me to follow my father's desire for peace in the Middle East. I am sitting around a table with my rabbis, an Egyptian-born priest of an Eastern Orthodox Christian Church, a Muslim from Pakistan, and American Jews and Israelis in a north-side Indianapolis hotel. The renewed violence in the Middle East has created new tensions even here in this city. We think we can overcome some of the distrust and anger that have separated our communities of faith if we can just sit down and talk. There are home-made cookies and baklava to sweeten what promises and proves to be a very hard conversation.

We choose to begin by learning more about each other. One of the participants is a Palestinian who has lived in Indianapolis for many years. He is chosen to tell us his story first, and I am to follow. Throughout his talk, the person to my left keeps refilling my water glass. My throat is dry. This is the story of my life.

My grandmother was born in Jerusalem in 1899. After meeting my grand-father, they moved to Haifa where my dad was born in an Arab neighborhood. From the time my great grandparents immigrated in Palestine, my family lived mostly among Arabs. Everyone was fluent in Arabic. My parents spoke of the good times they had with their Arab neighbors—the closeness, sharing, and respect.

Everything changed when Israel was proclaimed a state in 1948. My dad, an advocate for peace, was pulled into the fight against his Arab neighbors. He was shot several times and left for dead. It was a miracle that he survived. Yet he never gave up his belief that Arabs and Israelis could live together.

My own childhood was punctuated by terrorist attacks and bomb threats. I lost several family members in the Yom Kippur War in 1973 and many friends during the war with Lebanon in 1982. Still, my parents always told me that there are no winners in war. I studied Arabic in school and joined Shalom Achshav (Peace Now), where I formed close relationships with many Arab friends.

I'm in Indianapolis now. The quiet and calm I felt before September 11, 2001, has changed. In Israel, you check the news every half-hour just to be sure that no one you know has been injured or killed. Now, terror feels closer to my new Indianapolis home as well.

Now I teach preschool children at Congregation Beth-El Zedeck. The children come from different races and religions. I have come to this dialogue because I believe that, for the sake of the children, there is a way forward and there is hope.

I have experienced Indianapolis as laid back, friendly, and welcoming. And even today, harsh words do not break the rules of politeness. It's not at all like the Knesset, the Israeli Parliament; no one shouts, no one interrupts. Still, the conversation around the table lasts longer than planned. Difficult words are exchanged. My heart races, and my palms are sweaty. No one is thirsty, but we all take a few sips of water, and our hands grasp our glasses more tightly than necessary. There is significant disagreement, even here, far away from the fighting. Everyone has someone, a relative, a friend in the Middle East. Passions are strong. But a Hoosier propriety prevails that keeps anger in check. We will meet again. We have to. We can't give up.

Interview by Sandy Eisenberg Sasso

Tali Marotz came to Indianapolis with her husband and three children in December 1999. She is a preschool and Hebrew teacher and an artist.

A Conversation about Marriage

I went down to the Abbey to talk about gay life in Indianapolis with Rory Shivers and Ed Trout, but we ended up talking about marriage. Rory and Ed have been together six years, and, despite the fact that Indiana does not recognize same-sex unions, they, their families, and their friends consider themselves to be a married couple. Both men grew up in small-town Indiana—Rory in Marion, Ed in Greenfield; both cite their parents' long, happy marriages as models for their own.

They met in 1994, while performing in Footlite's production of *Best Little Whorehouse in Texas,* and immediately became friends; directly afterward, they were both cast in *Brigadoon.* "I fell in love with Ed then," Rory says. "I had only known him for about four months, but I knew. I was thirty-four. You know when you're in love at thirty-four." But Ed was involved with another man at the time, so Rory kept it to himself, fearful of losing the person who had become his best friend. Finally, a mutual friend said, "This is silly. You're eaten up inside, and you don't even know how he feels."

"I told Ed that we had to talk," Rory says. "I told him everything."

Ed wasn't sure how he felt, but Rory persisted. "I made Ed's life miserable for quite a while, because I was really in love with him. I kept telling him, 'It's going to happen.'"

In time, it did. And both of them agree that it's forever.

This kind of close, enduring marriage is what they've both always wanted. Both love being a part of each other's extended families as well. "We're lucky in that regard," Ed says. Both families are supportive of the marriage, treating Ed and Rory like any other married couple. They are active, involved uncles to ten nieces and nephews between them; recently, they shared a condo with Rory's family on a trip to Disney World.

Is it a perfect marriage? No.

"Every relationship has its bad points," Ed says. "No way around it."

"But it *is* for better or worse," Rory says.

"I guess it's because of the way I was brought up, but I don't get the way some people, if they're not having a great time, just move on," Ed says. "We have friends in good relationships, and there's this urge to cheat."

"This marriage is forever," Rory says, but adds, "Does that mean I'm not attracted to other people? For God's sake! I'm not dead. Ed knows that. But I'm not going to act on it. I love this man. I passionately love this man! And I love him more every day. I'll be frustrated; he'll be frustrated with me. But there's never been a time when I haven't loved him. Of course, we get on each other's nerves living together all the time. But we talk about it, work things out."

A same-sex union is no different, fundamentally, from a heterosexual one, they both agree. You have the same things to deal with every day of your life: bills to pay, chores to do. You have to balance your work and your social life; you must find the right balance of togetherness and solitude. Your sex life is only part of the mix—an important part, but not everything.

"And anybody's sex life is such a personal thing," Rory muses. "I never have been able to figure out why some people even care what other people do in bed. It so *doesn't* affect them."

I suggest that maybe people get hung up about gay sex life because there's this idea that all gay men are sexually promiscuous. Some are, some aren't—and isn't it mainly *young* gay men who are promiscuous? Aren't young people generally promiscuous, gay or straight? They are, both men agree. In fact, there's a wide range of sexual behavior in gays and straights of any age.

"But men are *designed* for sex," Rory says. "So when it's two men in a relationship," he laughs, "well, it's more on their minds." But he points out that if some young gay men go through a period of being wildly promiscuous, it may be at least partly because it's not socially acceptable for them to date. "Nobody gives them any sense of boundaries or standards," he says. "So it happens in the bars. It becomes all about sex."

It's better than it used to be, though. Both men cite IYG (Indiana Youth Group) that provides counseling services to gay teenagers and—most importantly—a place for them to *be* as a huge help. P-Flag, an organization of the parents of gay people of all ages, provides support to gay people and their families. And there's a greater general awareness, as well, which leads to greater tolerance and understanding.

As for Indianapolis? Both Rory and Ed like it here just fine. They're close to their families in Marion and Greenfield. They enjoy the active arts scene in town, particularly the excellent opportunities provided by community theater. They have a great circle of friends—both gay and straight. They feel comfortable in their workplaces.

Still, there are things they just don't do here—holding hands in public, for example—or making any other display of affection toward one another. It's just not acceptable in Indianapolis, they say in a matter-of-fact manner. And it can be dangerous. Gay bashings happen all the time.

Finding a church home has been another problem, particularly for Rory, who comes from a deeply religious family and would like to be involved with the kind of community of believers he knew as a child. "All kinds of people. Not just gays." But visiting local churches, too often the message he hears is about sin and condemnation. "I know the Bible," he says. "And it's not about condemnation. If homosexuality *were* a sin—which I don't believe it is—gay people should be welcomed and embraced by church congregations. When I go to a church and they start talking about homosexuality as a vile sin, it's time for me to leave."

Organized religion is less an issue for Ed, but he agrees that if they decide to have a commitment ceremony, it would be nice to have it in a church. They've just bought a house together, and it has a lovely garden. They could have the ceremony there. "But is that a good thing to do with respect to our neighbors?" Rory says. "A commitment ceremony between two men on the near east side of Indianapolis—does that open us up to hate crimes? We do have to be careful."

Interview by Barbara Shoup

❧

Rory Shivers is a systems trainer for Fifth Third Bank in Indianapolis and is active in community theater. He has performed at Civic and Edyvean Theaters.

Ed Trout is the co-owner and artistic director of National Comedy Theatre's Comedy Sportz and a freelance artist. He has performed at Theater on the Square and the Edyvean Theatre.

Our Kind Angels from God

Just before my husband and I left the Soviet Union to come to Indianapolis, we took a walk and sat down on a bench to read a newspaper. There, we were accosted by an anti-Semitic young man who yelled at us that we should die.

Still, we were afraid to leave and go to a strange country because we were old and sick. Before coming here, I was near death. For one year, my sickness chained me to the bed. Then I could walk only with crutches for nine months. I was walking with a cane when I came to Indianapolis.

Although we had heard of Washington, New York, and Chicago, Indianapolis was totally unknown to us. We thought that perhaps American Indians lived in this city. We couldn't believe that we were in America when we arrived because we didn't see buildings with ten or twenty floors. We thought that we had come to a village because the homes were small and there were cornfields all around. This couldn't be America!

But in America, we were met by beautiful volunteers. Their responsive hearts and careful hands made us happy. They provided us with food, drove us to the doctor, and taught us the English language. They were our guides to American life, our kind angels from God. We will never forget them.

We were welcomed by all. People of all religions were kind and pleasant to us. My reaction to this kindness was a desire to kiss everyone I met.

Once when my husband and I left our home, I felt a sharp pain in the belly. I couldn't go any further. I sat on the grass. My confused husband didn't know what to do. The street was empty—no people, no cars around. But like a miracle, one car appeared. The driver stopped, found out what happened, and drove us to the hospital. There, the doctor performed surgery and after five days, I was healthy and at home. Unfortunately, I didn't even know the name of this kind man who drove me to the hospital.

Shortly after we arrived in Indianapolis, we decided to go downtown to the Central Library by bus. We didn't know where the library was and asked the driver in very halting English to let us off at the library. The driver didn't speak to us, but instead used a telephone he had in the bus to make a call. At one point, the bus stopped and the driver motioned for us to get off. As we left the bus, we were greeted by a metro car and driven the very short distance to the library. The bus driver had called for the car to assist us. We were overcome at the kindness this total stranger had shown us.

Now our hearts are full to see the bar mitzvah of our grandson and to listen to him lead the songs and prayers of Shabbat. We feel America is our native country and Indianapolis our native city. God bless America. We thank God everyday; many, many times every day, we thank God.

Interview by Sharon Mishkin

꘎

Clara and Dimitri Bogolmony were both born in 1924 and lived in the Ukraine. They moved to Ekaterinburg in Siberia in 1982. Clara worked as a pediatrician and Dimitri as a military engineer. In 1990, they received an invitation from relatives to come to Indianapolis. They were active members and volunteers at Congregation Beth-El Zedeck. They recently moved to Boston, where their son was offered an opportunity for career advancement.

A Voluminous **Green Silk Dress**

On the morning after the Rodney King decision came down, setting free the policemen who had nearly beaten King to death during the Los Angeles riots, Broad Ripple High School's black students arrived at school enraged. They requested an assembly for the public expression of their anger and concern. The administration granted this very reasonable request, but made the mistake of limiting this expression to African-American students, thus instantly polarizing the student body. White, Asian, and Hispanic students, who felt equally angry and despairing about the decision, were deeply offended at being denied the opportunity to show support for their black classmates and share their own grief.

"I thought we were friends," one of my white students said to me.

"Don't they know we care, too?" said another.

Tension mounted. Fights broke out, threats were made, and we all were fearful about what might happen, not only in our own school, but everywhere, as our country processed its shock in the wake of this clear failure of our justice system.

I felt a little anxious myself driving to school the next morning to pick up my senior writers, who were going to attend the Christamore Writers' Luncheon with me. My heart sank when I turned the corner onto Broad Ripple Avenue and saw the fire truck, police cars, and news vans parked near the school's front entrance. I sat in my car a long moment, contemplating what might be happening inside, wondering if I would be wise to go home, call the Humanities and Performing Arts office, and make sure that it was safe to come in to collect my students. That's ridiculous, I told myself. This is my school, too. I belong here.

I got out of my car and started toward the front entrance. The side door, the one most convenient to our magnet office, is usually locked after all the students arrive in the morning; but, glancing toward it, I saw that there were two black girls standing there. They could hit the bar, unlock the door from the inside, and let me in—but would they? Maybe I should just go to the front entrance, I thought—just avoid dealing with the situation. I confess to a moment's hesitation, which still makes me feel ashamed, especially remembering the way one of those girls flung open the door as I approached and the other girl smiled and said, "Ooh, I love your dress!"

It was a wonderful voluminous green silk dress, and I was so filled with joy by the girls' friendliness that I laughed and twirled a little to make it fan out. "It's big enough for all of us," I said. "Want to get inside?" They laughed, too, and throughout the day I was so grateful to them for the reminder that assuming the worst and avoiding each other in troubled times, we risk losing the opportunity to make those small, pure human connections that make all the difference in our ability to get along.

Barbara Shoup

a new life has come among you

Children hold a city's future in their hands. What they learn at home, in school, and on the streets will shape the kind of adults they will become. As much as young singles choose to live in an urban center to be close to work and cultural activities, when those same people marry and begin families they often leave the city to make a "safer" life for their children.

Schools and city government document poor test scores and poverty; hospitals and courts report disturbing rates of teenage pregnancy and crime. But behind every number is the life of a child—and children don't often get to tell their life stories. In the next few pages, you will read the stories of young people, told by themselves, and the adults who teach them and care for them. They will take you into parochial school classrooms and public school hallways, to cheerleading tryouts and football fields, into emergency rooms and jail cells. There are alarming failures and some heartening successes. There are children who make it and those who don't live long enough for us to find out if they could.

When my daughter was in high school, her class was given an assignment to write about something interesting that happened when they were younger. She told me that one of her classmates reported that he was almost poisoned as a baby when his grandmother accidentally put cleaning fluid in his bottle. After reviewing a number of her growing-up experiences, my daughter concluded, in exasperation, that nothing very interesting ever happened to her. Perhaps a measure of a city's success may just be how few "interesting" stories our children have to tell.

A new life has come among you.
Make its path smooth—
then shall it travel beyond the four hills!

—Omaha Tribe

Busted

Very early on a summer morning in the early sixties, I am awakened by my friends Gus, Tom, and Larry in the alley below my bedroom window. They're on their bikes, out looking for bundles of comic books left on drugstore stoops by overnight deliverymen. It has become something of a sport for some kids around Fountain Square, filching these helpless hot goods. We do not know that the cops have noticed this also. I can go with the guys, make the grab, and be clear in time for my paper route.

Late on a summer morning in the early nineties, I awaken a lady named Pamela Johnson by knocking on her door on a two-block-long street called Harvard Place, near Crown Hill Cemetery. She is clutching a bathrobe across the front of her body. I am holding a notebook. I am from the newspaper, and I want to ask her about her fifteen-year-old son, Ronald, who has just been sentenced to 170 years in prison for murdering two of their neighbors, eighty-three and eighty-seven years old. Ronald was thirteen when he and a companion killed them, the sisters Julia Bellmar and Anna Harris. The boys entered the ladies' house because they wanted money to go to the state fair. Now, other neighbors talk to the newspaperman about reinforcing their locks and buying guns. "They know I'm the mother of the kid who did it," Pamela Johnson says quietly in her doorway. "That doesn't make me a bad person."

In the late morning, I wait with my friends Gus, Tom, and Larry in what is called the bullpen, a caged section of the old police station just north of Virginia Avenue on Alabama Street. Our bikes have been impounded. The contents of our wallets have been dropped into large yellow envelopes. Gus jokes that he did his image no good, getting caught with playing cards on top of everything else. I keep my fear at bay until I see my father in his gray workpants striding along the gray wood floor. We were always forbidden even to telephone him at the shop, and now I have made him take time off to get me out of jail. This is an emergency.

On a fine spring morning in the early nineties, I sit in a courtroom with my notebook, watching the smooth, alert face of Ahmad Foster, a fifteen-year-old boy wearing a baggy print shirt and undergoing prosecution for shooting to death a seventy-eight-year-old woman at a bus stop because she would not let him have her purse. He and his two brothers split $105 from Mildred Stansfield, who had caught their attention because she was wearing a red coat that December day, honoring Christmas. I watch, later, in the corridor during a recess, as Ahmad Foster's mother and grandmother approach Mildred Stansfield's sister and take her hands in theirs. All three women may be dead before Ahmad is free again.

In the late summer or early fall, my father and I take the bus to 25th Street and Keystone Avenue for our final meeting with the juvenile court administrator, who sees us in an office rather than a courtroom. I tell the man yes, I have learned my lesson, I have committed no crimes since the botched comic book heist, and I understand that you don't just take someone else's property without asking. My father and I both sit with hands folded between our knees. I know something that I do not say, and perhaps would not have words for, and that is, I want very much never to do anything that forces me to see my father look like this again.

On an afternoon in the middle nineties, I am sitting with several correctional staff, a sign language interpreter, and an inmate of the Indiana Women's Prison named Kimberly McDowell. She will be released soon, having served thirteen years for burning down a house with several members of her foster family inside. A child died in the fire. Kimberly was sixteen when she did it, angry over some disciplinary incident nobody can remember. She was found to be mentally ill also, but was sent to prison anyway. She is deaf. Her fingers flutter as I watch her lowered eyes and listen to her interpreter and write my notes. She is ready to leave prison, she says; but she is frightened also of going back to the world. She is thirty, and she still misses her father, who disappeared many years ago. It was him she was looking for when the authorities found her on the streets of Fort Wayne, at age thirteen or fourteen, and put her in foster care. "I have many nightmares," her fingers spell out. "I asked my friend to bring a crucifix to help me. I have nightmares again. Sometimes, I feel okay. Sometimes I feel fine. Maybe my father is holding me."

The early seventies, very late on a Saturday night. I am in the white light of the modern police headquarters in the City-County Building, telling a detective that my sister's boyfriend has taken her away holding a gun to her head. The detective is friendly but cannot do anything for us. My father is at home. He will find out from her, eventually, in a hurried phone call, that she is all right. Had he gone to police headquarters, it would have been the first time since the early sixties, when he was the father of a kid in trouble and had to get down there and do something about it.

Dan Carpenter

Those Who **Rose Above**

In a way, prejudice brought me to the Indianapolis Public School system. When I finished at Butler, I wanted to be a football coach. I tried for a job in Greenwood. I tried in Westfield. What I encountered was, believe it or not, problems with being Catholic and having an Italian name and coming from the East. I didn't think that was a factor whatsoever in being considered for a school position, but I found out in both places that it was. You dealt with the trustee then, of course, and I had one trustee tell me, "We'd love to have somebody with your background and the coaching, but people here would never accept anybody like that." I found out, as I checked around the state, that it was pretty much like that in Indiana if you went outside the cities. So I figured I'd better stick with the city.

Today, anybody who so much as hints that he wants to coach can get a position easily, at least as an assistant. But back then, there was quite a waiting list to get in the high schools. So I took a position as coach of all sports and physical education teacher at School 76, which then had a principal who was against athletics. The first thing he said to me was, "I understand you want to have football here, and I'm here to tell you we're not going to have football. Our kids are too small and too weak." So I was stuck that year. But the next year, I talked him into having a football team and we did very well. Didn't lose a game. I had no trouble after that.

In 1961, I became a high school football coach. Harry E. Wood High School was started in 1953 as the 11th high school in IPS, and it became the site for special education when that was in its embryonic stages. Wood became the place where the other high schools found a way to send their special education kids. Under Richard Emery, a principal who became nationally known, they started lots of the vocational programs that are now popular throughout the country— auto body, service station, restaurant management, horticulture, shoe repair, cleaning and pressing, hairdressing. But it was kind of a dumping ground. Maybe 60 percent of our enrollment was special ed and borderline academically. The other schools didn't know what to do with them.

Most of the kids came from very negative environments, where if there was any kind of a family, it was a family living in great risk—alcoholism, lots of physical as well as sexual abuse. The kids came and went. The rest of the city wasn't bad yet; we didn't have the great exodus taking place. But Wood was probably the precursor of what was going to occur for all of IPS.

A story comes to my mind that might highlight this period. I had one kid, a Caucasian kid, who was only a sophomore and quickly reached a level where he was going to be one of our best players of all time, offensively and defensively. One day at practice—we practiced down at Garfield Park because we had no practice facility—right in the middle of practice, here comes a police car. A big policeman gets out, stops my practice, comes up to me, and says, "I got to have that boy right there."

I said, "What do you mean, you got to have that boy?"

He said, "That boy is the father of the baby that my daughter had last week." And he says, "I want him now, he's coming with me."

And I say, "Wait a minute. I'm responsible for him. He belongs here. If there's some reason that he has to go elsewhere or not be associated with us, I'll look into it."

And he says, "No," and he puts his hand kind of where—I wouldn't say he was going for his gun, that would be exaggerating—but he was making it be known how serious he was. So we've stopped the practice, all the team members are watching as he and I are having a face to face, and he says, "I'm taking that boy whether you want it or not, and you try and stop me."

His story was that this fifteen- or sixteen-year-old kid had fathered his daughter's child, and he needed to get out of school and quit playing games like football, and get a job. Well, I resisted; but I couldn't stop a police officer who was threatening. He was going to charge me with interfering with him. I tried to tell the guy, "You know, if you want a good future for your daughter, if they're going to be together, he's got to stay in school, he's got to graduate, he's got to have a chance for a decent future."

He had no sense. He wouldn't listen. He took the kid by the collar—with all his football equipment and uniform—and shoved him into his car. I never saw that kid again.

That's not to say there weren't success stories. We did a good job there—not just myself, but all of us—in getting kids into colleges. It's just that so many of them came from such negative home environments, where there just wasn't any encouragement to succeed or even to go to school. There were those who did not make it. They fell to the drug influence. They're no longer living.

And there were those who rose above.

About two years ago, my wife and I were at the airport on our way to Venice for a Mediterranean cruise, and someone tapped me on the shoulder. I turned around to see an athlete I had in the early sixties. I could still recognize him. He told me he was now a chemist at Lilly, and he and his wife were on their way for a twenty-one-day vacation on the Nile River.

He said, "You know, Mr. Caporale, I have never forgotten when you were talking to the team about doing well in school and thinking about ways to be a worthwhile person and being able to raise a family well and be the right kind of citizen. And I remember how you were talking to the whole team and you mentioned me"—his name was Bob Murff, he was a starting halfback on the football team—"and while you were talking to the team like that, you looked right at me, and you said, 'More of you should be doing like Bob, really working to succeed in school so that you can amount to something.' You made me feel so good."

To tell you the truth, I gave so many talks I don't remember saying it, but he said, "I never forgot that."

Interview by Dan Carpenter

❧

Lou Caporale (1932–2001) of rural Greenwood was a teacher, coach, and administrator in Indianapolis Public Schools for thirty-five years, retiring in 1990. A New Jersey native of Italian descent, he lived in this area for forty-five years.

Growing Up **Catholic**

On the day after Labor Day in 1931, my mother escorted me to the first grade classroom at Cathedral Grade School, where we were greeted by Sister Columba, a short, stout woman encased in the standard garb of the Sisters of Providence—black, floor-length habit with starched white linen breastplate. She was wearing sensible black shoes. Her hair was concealed beneath a tight-fitting black and white wimple. Hanging from her waist was a massive rosary.

She seemed cheerful enough when we arrived. But in the first hour, she called me to the front of the room and promptly shoved the back of my head against the blackboard, giving the class its first lesson: Behave here, or incur my wrath. I never did learn whether I had been disciplined for some infraction or whether I was simply the tool she used to set her ground rules.

I survived, as did most of my classmates at the school at 14th and Pennsylvania streets, a mile and a half north of downtown. For the next twelve years, our lives revolved around that place and Cathedral High School and St. Agnes Academy; all three grouped near SS. Peter & Paul Cathedral, seat of the Archdiocese of Indianapolis.

As to Sister Columba's skull session, I don't remember whether I even bothered to report the incident to my parents. I knew, even at the age of six, that the Church—nuns and priests and brothers—could do no wrong in my mother's eyes. How could a mother not think kindly of the nuns when their sons brought home letters like this one that I penned in the first grade and my mother saved for nearly a half century:

"I am glad that your feast day comes next Sunday. May is Mary's month. Mary is our heavenly Mother. You are my earthly Mother. God gave you to me. I think He gave me the best Mother in the whole world. I shall always love my two sweet Mothers." What did it matter that the same letter went to every other mother of a first grader?

The building of character permeated our lives. We were in school to make something of ourselves. Sloth was to be avoided, because idle hands were the devil's workshop. Sex was to be enjoyed only during marriage and solely for procreation.

This last prohibition made boy-girl relationships a bit strained. My sister Sally remembered that girls and boys in the eighth grade would meet on Sunday afternoons at the Cinema Theater on 16th Street for the 1:30 movie and then head for the cathedral for vesper services. "But we always split up before we got to church. The boys would go in one door and we girls in another. We never wanted the sisters to know we had been together."

The vigilance was effective. I can't recall any girl in high school getting pregnant. Abortion was an unthinkable option. Divorce was considered scandalous, if not tragic.

We believed what the nuns taught us about heaven and hell. It wasn't until well into adulthood that we began questioning the many articles of faith that had been drilled into us. We were living in the twilight of the Victorian Age. Few adults hugged or kissed in public. I sometimes think it was the heavy emphasis on the hazards of sex that made it difficult for so many people to be intimate with the opposite sex. I don't ever remember seeing my parents, or my friends' parents, embrace. Parents and children seldom mentioned that they loved each other, though it was always implied.

In those days, we were warned repeatedly about the evils of materialism, a warning most of us felt comfortable with because we had so little of the world's goods anyway. "The difference between being rich and poor during the Depression," my older brother Bill once remarked, "was a five-dollar bill."

Still, we never felt deprived. And even though the Ku Klux Klan, which had ruled the state in the twenties, had targeted Catholics even more than Jews and blacks, we led such sheltered lives that most of the children at Cathedral were unaware of the anti-Catholicism all around us. Some of the bolder non-Catholic kids referred to us as "cat lickers," but usually they were racing away as they yelled it.

The Cathedral parish was booming in those years. The directory listed 4,500 souls. Fifty years later, there were fewer than five hundred. The grade school became so crowded in my childhood that grades five through eight were taught in a frame house across the alley. After World War II, when the parishioners began to abandon the parish for the suburbs, the house had many uses, including a clubhouse for young Catholic singles and finally as a soup kitchen for the homeless. The grade school where the nuns warned us of the hazards of sex has become the Damien Center for AIDS patients.

Lawrence S. Connor

A Pair of **Fat Pants**

Step. Step. Step. Tuuurrrrnnn. . . .

I don't remember whose idea it was, but I do remember how, once expressed, the rightness of it settled over me, comfortable as a pair of fat pants. I would audition for the Pacemates—as a joke, of course—and write about it. I mentioned the idea to my sister, Jenny, who had just finished her third year as a Pacemate; stricken, she nearly choked on her Caffeine Free Diet Coke.

Then she offered this gentle advice: "No offense, but you might want to lose a bit of weight first." I pondered this as I nibbled on cake and decided that she was right. If I was going to audition, even if I was just kidding around, I had to be believable. So I gave up soda. Then, for good measure, I tanned extensively and dyed my hair a coquettish shade of blonde. About a week before the audition, in an act of desperation, I started jogging; sadly, the effects were negligible.

When the big day arrived, I was forced to rely on excessively tight-fitting flesh-colored hosiery to subtract from my ample thighs. The tights weren't enough. When I entered Market Square Arena for the tryouts, I realized I outweighed nearly everyone in the room (and, mind you, it's a big room) by a good thirty pounds. I stepped my way through the standard freak-me-out skinny girls with big obnoxious hair, improbable fingernails, and body glitter, most of whom were busy limbering up, and planted myself next to my sister. Slouched comfortably, she chatted up her fellow Pacemate alums, while I rifled through the chipper introductory packet I had received at the door. I carefully pinned my bib number over my lower abs (a problem area), and eavesdropped on a discussion of the relative weight-loss benefits of diabetes versus those of catching strep and mono at the same time. After extensive sitting around, we were taught our first move: The Sexy Walk. It went like this: Step. Step. Step. Step. Tuuurrrnnn, Tuuurrrnnn. Repeat. I thought I'd be able to handle this, but when it was my turn to do it in front of the group, I tripped. I caught myself—there was no falling. But there it was, a blemish on my record. Thankfully, the choreographer, Monique, was forgiving, and I lived to see round two. (Okay, what really happened was that Monique and I had an agreement: I would remain in the audition all day, through all three rounds, whether I deserved to or not, so that I could experience the full brunt of rejection for the sake of powerful journalism.)

Round two was where things really started to fall apart. I learned the first part of the routine, which consisted of about eight counts, and figured I'd be okay. But then Monique went on to teach us about ten additional parts, and that's where I lost it. There were triple pirouettes. There was rolling on the floor. There were high kicks and dramatic, Edvard Munchian gestures. Eventually, I had to perform this hellish combination with only two other girls to shield me from the 150 pairs of eyes in the room. Alas, my comrades were as clueless as I; dashed were my hopes of simply copying the moves made by the girl next to me.

So the music started, and I got through the first six counts or so, flailed around a bit, and gave up. Sympathetic to my plight (and understanding the special circumstances surrounding my attendance of the audition), Monique restarted the music. This time I remembered even fewer steps, and trudged shamefacedly toward the gaggle of girls who watched from the edge of the floor. "Do you want to try it again?" asked Monique's tinny voice over the loudspeaker. Embarrassed, I whined, "See, the thing is, *none* of us know what we're doing, so we can't, like, *cue* off each other." Ever patient, she offered to cue us from her perch in the bleachers, but even this kindness was not enough; we only continued to flail. But then—O miracle!—it came to me: I remembered the last half of the combination! I hurled myself to the floor, rolled around, righted myself, did some kicks, and spun around a few times. The conclusion of my performance was heralded with loud applause from the gallery—bestowed out of pity, no doubt.

As I swigged from my water bottle, Jenny said—in that enthused tone that people use to exclaim how cute a baby is when, in reality, it's hideously ugly—"That was good to pick it up in the middle like that!" Then she shed her warm-ups and strode to the center of the floor. Within seconds, she had caught the attention of every person in the room. She was perfect. She hit every kick, nailed every turn. She was coy. She was sexy. When she finished, every soul in attendance clapped and meant it.

That's when I began to realize that there's more to this Pacemating stuff than I thought. After all, it's not like I'd never taken a dance lesson—I began studying ballet at age six and took classes off and on (okay, mostly off) until my freshman year in high school. But as I watched, it occurred to me that some of these women had dedicated large parts of themselves to dancing. Not only that, but they all have real lives, too—frankly, the salary of $40 per game doesn't pay the bills. My sister is a lawyer. Another alum is an executive at a staffing service. One girl lives and works in Louisville (Kentucky!) and drives to Indianapolis for every practice and game.

When I considered what each one sacrifices (not counting food) just to be a part of the whole Pacemate thing, my auditioning didn't seem so funny anymore, because what I had been doing was mocking these women—including my sister, whom I adore with every ounce of my being (and God knows my being has plenty of ounces).

To be honest, I was glad when I was cut after only the second round (contrary to my agreement with Monique). But here's the killer: I was also just a smidgen disappointed because—I can't believe I'm actually admitting this—it had occurred to me during those long soda-free weeks before the audition that it might be neat if, by some miracle, I managed to make the squad. I had let myself imagine what it must be like to be so beautiful, to capture the attention of an arena filled with fans, but most of all to spend a season alongside my sister, being part of something she loves.

Kate Shoup Welsh

Class Rings and **Sock Gum**

The day he gave me the sock gum, our friendship began. It was still warm enough outside for shorts because he had a pair on. I remember. We had been in classes together the year before, but our relationship involved occasional hellos or shared laughs that were forgotten in minutes. I don't think he even knew my name. And we definitely weren't "sock friends."

Then Mike and I got assigned to the same homeroom. He sat in front of me in the third seat from the front—third row, third seat. I was in the fourth. There was a rule in our homeroom that you could only talk on Fridays. So throughout the week, we talked before the bell rang and then in whispers during class. On Fridays, we talked aloud.

On what I now call "Sock Day," sometime during the first week of school, I came in and sat in my seat behind him and asked if he had any gum. "I only have one piece left, but I'll give it to you since you're my friend," Mike answered cheerfully. He reached down and pulled a piece of Winterfresh from his sock. I must have looked at him kind of crazy, because he smiled and said, "You know, you should feel very special. I only give my good friends sock gum. You're lucky that we're so close." I laughed. Instantly, he had made me feel like I belonged.

One day, we got yelled at for whispering in class, so Mike decided to draw something to keep himself occupied. What would he draw? That day he had worn two T-shirts, and the outer one had a cartoon figure on its back. With a surge of inspiration, he turned the T-shirt around so that the figure was on his front. Then he got an even better idea. Removing the shirt, Mike spread it out before him and began to sketch. At the end of period, he proudly displayed a duplicate of the cartoon on his shirt. It was some kind of goblin with large, floppy ears, a big grin, a really skinny body, and a large head.

The next time he wore that shirt, I was bored. Because he sat in front of me, I began to sketch the figure myself. I must have done a pretty good job, because he smiled and told me that I had done well. Now I wish I had kept that sketch . . . kind of.

Days, weeks, and months went by, and Mike and I had serious talks when circumstances permitted. It's strange, but I remember them all. Maybe I worried about what he said and wanted to help him grasp his dreams. Maybe it was the enthusiasm in his voice when he shared them with me. He had such high hopes for his future.

Mike wasn't an angel. He smoked cigarettes, got high, and said that he had done acid once. But when he spoke of these things, he used to say, "I'm going to quit. I'm going to straighten up my life." One time, he told me he was afraid of going to jail for getting into trouble with some friends. He was in tears. He knew that if he went to jail, his whole life would be thrown away.

"I'm young. I'm only eighteen," he kept saying. "These are my times to have fun. When I get older, it will be time to be serious. It's not bad to party now . . . is it? I should get it out of my system, so that I can settle down and be good when I'm older. About twenty-five is a good age to settle down, huh? Yeah, I'll act responsible when I'm twenty-five. There's plenty of time."

One day, he was all excited. "Hey, Alissa! We just got through having this really cool guest speaker in ROTC."

"Really? What was he talking about?"

"He told us about how he used to be wild when he was my age. He used to party and do the same things I do. When he got out of high school, he went into the Army and from there he was placed into a special leadership program where he helps out teens. That sounds really cool, huh? I could do that, you know. I would be really cool with teens. I would respect them and then when I told them what to do, it wouldn't seem like I was bossing them because we would be cool. I could get my life together. That guy did. I'm going to try to do that."

"That sounds great, Mike! You should do it!"

Sometimes, he counseled me on relationship problems even though he didn't have a special girl himself. "Man, you won't believe what my boyfriend did," I complained once. "It was before the class that he and I have together. He was talking with his friends, and I was talking with mine. But the next thing I know, I look over at him, and he is flinging one of the girls around in circles over his head. They looked like a pair of happy ballerinas practicing a routine. Just the day before, that girl had been telling everyone how much he loved her. I felt like a fool!"

"Well, maybe he doesn't consider that flirting," Mike grinned. "Maybe he just has secret ambitions to be a ballerina!" My friend was always like that. He always tried to get me to see my boyfriend's point of view and help me understand the crooked "boy way of thinking."

When the time came for seniors to get information about caps and gowns, senior books, announcements, pictures, and class rings, Mike was really excited. "I'm going to get a ring, and that means I get my cap and gown free," he announced as he showed me a catalog full of senior items. He pointed out which color rock he would choose for his ring and was trying to figure out which sides to pick. Mike also wanted a '99 key chain. "My class ring is going to be 'tight,'" he decided, and he told me that he was ready to graduate and be out of high school.

One homeroom day will stay etched in my memory forever. It was on a Monday, and Mike came in and sat down in front of me. The bell hadn't rung, so he turned around and gave me his cheery hello. His weekend had been on "chill," he said, and he hadn't done much partying. He was having a good day. The bell rang, and the class got quiet because we weren't allowed to talk.

I noticed that Mike had on our doodling shirt. I spent the rest of the period spaced out, staring at that funny little cartoon on his back. When the bell rang, we said good-bye and parted. On most days, I said, "Bye, Mike. Be good." But on that Monday, I didn't.

The next morning, my mother woke me to watch the news. A Broad Ripple student had been murdered the night before, she said. "Some boy from ROTC."

I was nonchalant. I was calm. Students from my school had died before . . . either by accident or from being shot. It was always someone I didn't know. Then the news came on. "A Broad Ripple ROTC student was killed on the east side last night . . ."

Mike was in ROTC. Mike lived on the east side. Terrified, I started pleading with the television, "Not Mike. Not Mike. Not Mike. Please not Mike."

The reporter continued, "Mike L. was shot to death in an east-side alley last night, allegedly after an argument over a girl. Mike was a senior at Broad Ripple High School and would have graduated in June."

"No! No!" I screamed. And then I began to weep.

Alissa Cook

Shelter for **Devron**

In my second year of tutoring at Indianapolis Public School 83 at 42nd and Emerson, I met a little boy named Devron, who was seven years old. The teacher did not particularly like him. Clearly, he had some sort of learning disability. I loved that little boy with a passion. His five-year-old sister, Angel, was in kindergarten. Devron and Angel lived with their grandmother on 42nd Street in my neighborhood. Their grandmother had two jobs. She was home when the children came home from school to spend some time with them and cook them a hot supper. Then she went to her night job.

I got a number of my friends to spend some time with the kids in school. A doctor friend and a musician friend would sit on the floor with the children and tell them about their work. Devron was very drawn by these visitors. He was starved for affirmation. His mother was addicted to heroine. His grandmother did not let her daughter come into the house.

I had a Christmas party at my house for the children in the class. I strong-armed the principal into letting me do it. Actually, I shamed her. The principal had made a terrible mistake with me. She never called me back after four attempts of my offering help. Then she said, "We don't have volunteers in the

school. I know by the end of the second week in school which students will fail."
That was so incredibly offensive to me—that the person who was in charge of
the school could say that the littlest ones who come in there were already in a
box with her. Basically, that was the atmosphere in the school.

The teacher, whom I liked personally, never had control over the classroom. She was woefully ill equipped to teach elementary school. She didn't
know how to spell. She would misspell words on the blackboard when she was
copying from a book in her hand. She had a master's degree in teaching. It
made me wonder about our higher education system for teachers. I liked her
very much, and she liked the children. But she never gave the sense that she
was in charge.

The last week before Christmas vacation, Devron was not in school. I had
Christmas presents for him, so I took them home with me. The school was unable to get in touch with the grandmother until the last day before vacation.
One night while she was at work, her daughter and the current boyfriend had
taken both children out of the house crying. She couldn't find them. The daughter often slept in a car.

I got all the information I could, through the teacher, from Devron's file.
I'm sure it was quite illegal, but I got the grandmother's address and phone
number. I called the grandmother over Christmas break, gave her my phone
number, and said that I would be willing, no matter what, to help. After Christmas, I heard from Devron's grandmother. She had just received a call at her work
from the Holy Family Shelter. Devron and Angel were there. She had two hours
to pick them up, or they would go to child welfare. She said to me, "If you can
get to the shelter and tell them I'm coming, I'll get there. I will find someone to
drive me there."

I put the Christmas presents I had saved for Devron in the car and drove to
the Holy Family Shelter. I was furious at the mother. When I arrived at the shelter,
Devron and Angel weren't there. I strong-armed the woman at the shelter who
told me that they were at the elementary school nearby.

I went to Devron's classroom. The door was closed, but I opened it and
went in. He saw me immediately. I will never forget that as long as I live. He got
out of his seat and hurled himself at me. We sat on the floor of the hall, and he
just sobbed. I cried, too.

I told him that his grandmother was coming to get him. He asked, "Is she going to get Angel, too?"

"Yes," I answered.

I told Devron I had his Christmas presents from the class and from me. He asked, "Did you bring one for Angel?" I hadn't.

He responded, "Don't worry, I'll give her mine."

I called the teacher from his elementary school and told her what had happened to Devron. "You know," she told me, "this happens all the time."

I said, "I know." I know that in my head.

Devron returned to his regular school again until April. Then his mother came to get him, and they disappeared. I called the police. I talked to the police investigators. They said, "Mrs. Jones, this happens every day in the city."

Interview by Sandy Eisenberg Sasso

꙾

Anne Shelburne Jones came to Indianapolis in 1977. She is a teacher and spiritual director for the Episcopal Church and a member of St. Albans.

Someone Has Murdered This Child

There was once a little boy named Damien Johnson who came into the emergency room. This was one of the turning cases in my life, in my religious life. My son Max was about three years old, and my son Eli was one.

The hospital got a call from Tudor Lake Apartments that they were bringing in a two-year-old African-American child who was in full cardiac arrest. As I started to examine this child, I realized that he was covered with scratches and bite marks, cigarette burns, cuts, and bruises. There was every conceivable degree of abuse. I did CPR and we had a breathing tube in his lung, but it didn't make a difference; the child died.

The police report said that the mother's boyfriend called the ambulance and said the boy was choking. The boyfriend tried to make himself out to be the big hero. That is pretty much a description of someone who has committed a homicide in an abuse case. In real accidents, parents don't know what to do. They say it's all their fault. But this guy is trying to show how he was a real hero.

So I went back into the room to tell the mother that the child died. The boyfriend was there, too. So I said, "I'm sorry, but Damien is dead."

They all started screaming, and the boyfriend put his head in his hands. Then he put his hand on me. I remember how sickened I felt. I did not want this guy to touch me.

He asked, "How did Damien die, how did he die?"

I turned, looked at him, and said, "Someone has murdered this child. Do you know who might have murdered him?"

He said, "No, no, I don't know who did this." Then he added, "Wait a minute, maybe it's his mother's cousin."

He kept trying to touch me and talk to me. A male nurse was with me, and we were all distraught. The nurse saw me getting madder and madder. I kept slapping the boyfriend's arm off mine. I just did not want to be touched by this filth. I've never felt that way before. I've never felt that I was in the presence of pure filth and evil or that a human being could be like that. He sent a shiver through my whole soul. The nurse pulled me out into the waiting room because he thought I was going to lose it. So I calmed down and finished the rest of my shift.

That night I went home and climbed into bed with my three-year-old who was about the same age as Damien, and I promised that I would never lay a hand on him as long as I lived. I slept with him the entire night. I made a commitment that I would say Kaddish (a Jewish memorial prayer) for that little boy every night for at least a year. I figured that if nobody else loved the kid, at least I could do my part.

Interview by Sandy Eisenberg Sasso

𝓧

Louis Profeta has been Staff Emergency Physician at St. Vincent Hospital since 1994. He is co-founder of ERASE, Emergency Room Advice, Safety, and Education, a public safety awareness program for children.

Notes on a Failed Suicide

When the body hangs in a noose for several hours, the neck stretches like taffy twisted at the fair. We find them dangling from the barely lit basement, the tool shed, the disheveled closet. As a rule, I never converse with the dead. They remain politely silent while the coroner examines for lividity. From behind the sofa cushions, I etch names, birth dates, and phone numbers into a black notebook. Mom dials the aunt from out of town. I pace the kitchen tile until the chaplain arrives.

Sometimes, though, the dead walk up to you. Dialogue is never easy.

There was the time I was patrolling the west side on a cloudless afternoon, and my radio told me a young man had just jumped off the Morris Street Bridge into the White River. As the siren crooned and the lights awakened, I sped to assess the damage. I'd driven over that span a hundred times during my eight years in the Indianapolis Police Department. My notebook hugged my navy blue uniform as I began to calculate the distance the undertow would drag the body. I figured we'd begin searching beneath the metallic air of the chemical refinery to the south.

Arriving first at the scene, I was met by the frantic waving of a woman motorist.

"He's walking up the bank now!"

My glance caught a drenched boy breaking the thin tree line. I was too stunned to reach for my notebook. The fifty-foot plunge into the surging currents was as deadly as any rope or cord I had ever cut from a corpse's throat. The surface of the waterway can act like a smooth slab of cement bouncing a dime.

"Are you all right?"

"Cold, but okay," he responded, clutching his damp shoulder blades. "I never touched bottom. The current is strong, though."

Blood trickled from both his wrists. The clean incisions suggested the deed was performed with a fresh razor blade. This sixteen-year-old wanted to die; he had cut himself before falling over the railing. I didn't know how to respond to such a desperate act. I began to fill the lines in my notebook. No sofa or table to hide behind.

"Your back can snap at that height," I blurted.

No response.

"Can I call your mom? Tell her you're alive?"

His fragile frame was strapped to an ambulance gurney.

"Mom lives across town. I stay with my grandmother, but I'm too much for her to handle. She's been real sick lately anyway. Don't bother her."

"Is your dad at work? I'll get hold of him."

"We don't talk."

Nor could I, suddenly. The distance between the ambulance doors narrowed as a clear mask slid over the boy's face like a belated diving bell. Then the city's din swallowed him.

Greg Weber

What You Got to Learn

Yard Bird!" Paco slurred in his Howard Cosell voice, as if he were announcing the start of a championship fight.

"What? I'm only five minutes late, man. Give me a break," I pleaded. "All I'm missing is English."

"You missin' mo' than that, son. And now you doin' Bird Duty!" he announced as his huge puffy fist—one that had slammed prison bars closed and cuffed lifers around at the Pendleton Reformatory during his job as a guard there—stuffed a work slip into my hand. Then he looked away, seeking his next delinquent. "So many Yard Birds to clean up that trashy Meridian Street lawn today," he muttered. "You guys must love Bird Duty. You better, 'cause you on it today!"

"By the way, Perry," he continued without turning his five-hundred-gallon-oil-drum-of-a-body around to me. "You late for mo' than English. Southerland has one of my former inmates coming to scare your little white ass straight today."

"Oh, great," I thought as I made my way through the dusty hallway of Shortridge High School. Usually, I would skip this class and meet a friend in the "bomb shelter" for a cigarette. Or we would write messages on paper planes and launch them like origami bottle rockets from the ledge outside of Ms. Repass' entomology room on the top floor.

From there, we could see James Whitcomb Riley's grave site. We felt we were higher than even this small Parthenon atop the Acropolis-like mount in nearby Crown Hill Cemetery. From there, we felt like we were above everything and, in a way, we were. Our feet dangled over "Science," "Education," "Painting," "Philosophy," and "Poetry," words that were engraved in the stone frieze above the great Corinthian column tops that composed the stately entrance to this school—an institution whose cavernous ducts we used like escape routes from a prison camp.

But today Paco's stern voice got to me. His reference to prison scared me, and I decided to head to class. On my way up the stairs to the English classroom, I saw Kevin running. He was late, too. He told me, in the chopped-up breath of a runner, that today's visitor to the school's Creative Writing Program was Etheridge Knight, a poet who had spent the last ten years in prison for armed robbery.

"Cool," I said. "He's got a great book out called *Poems from Prison*."

Just then Knight and his host, another poet named Jared Carter, came around the corner. Immediately, I noticed that Knight had scars. I imagined that they had come from his years on "the inside," where tattooed arms guard lunch trays, and hand signals and cigarettes are currency of the day.

As soon as we walked in the classroom, a half smile pushed the scar off his cheek, and I saw Knight take a cigarette out from behind his ear and put it in his suit coat pocket. Then he pulled out of a beaten-up briefcase what looked like a stack of newspapers.

After Carter introduced him to the class of ten students, Knight came straight to the point. Why were we interested in poetry? I told him I was just happy not to be in my English lit class and that I wasn't a good writing student because I didn't like how it was taught.

"What poets have you heard of? Which ones do you like?" he asked.

"Gwendolyn Brooks," I answered.

Knight stared at me for a long moment as a cloud crossed between our school and the sun, its shadow filling the room and turning his skin almost turquoise. He turned to his stack of papers on the desk and picked up a small paperback book. It was his *Poems from Prison*. He pointed to the introduction. It was written by Gwendolyn Brooks.

As he leaned to give me the book, it was almost as if he had opened a bottle of Jack Daniels whiskey and held the bottle top to my nose for me to smell it. He stood back and smiled.

That day, we watched Knight create poetry on the blackboard and then listened to him read a few of his poems. When he asked if we had any "questions, comments, or confrontations," I volunteered that I never knew where to start when writing a poem. I told him that usually they just come to me and that I don't know quite what to do with them.

"What can I read to figure this out?" I asked.

"What you got to learn about poetry, Arone," he answered in his slow Mississippi drawl, "ain't in no textbook. You have to live a little to learn to write. Life'll teach you what you want to say if you listen to it."

Aaren Yeatts Perry

Sandy Eisenberg Sasso has been rabbi at Congregation Beth-El Zedeck in Indianapolis since 1977. She lectures at Christian Theological Seminary and Butler University. She is the author of many articles on women and children's spirituality and of eight children's books. Two of her books, *But God Remembered* and *A Prayer for the Earth,* were selected as best books of the year by *Publisher's Weekly.* Her essays have appeared in the *Women's Torah Commentary; Jewish Lights; Falling toward Grace* (Indiana University Press); *Spiritual Education: Cultural, Religious, and Social Differences; New Perspectives for the Twenty-First Century;* as well as other publications. She writes a monthly column in the *Indianapolis Star.* Her book *Cain and Abel: Finding the Fruits of Peace* was published in fall 2001.

Nancy N. Baxter taught English and history at the high school and college level for twenty-three years. She is the author of seven books on Civil War and Indiana history. Her historical novel *Lords of the Rivers* won the National Federation of Presswomen's award for best historical novel. Baxter's essays have been featured in *Falling toward Grace* (Indiana University Press), the Indiana Historical Society's magazine *Traces, ISM Magazine,* and other periodicals. She is the 2000 winner of the Eli Lilly Lifetime History Achievement Award from the Indiana Historical Society.

S. L. Berry is a staff writer for the *Indianapolis Star,* where he covers the visual arts. He has written for numerous national publications and is the author of ten nonfiction books for children, young adults, and adults. The New York Public Library designated his biography of photographer/writer/film director Gordon Parks as one of 1992's best books for teens. Among his credits are *For the Sake of Art: The History of the Indianapolis Art Center* and a series of biographies on American poets for young people. He also provides writing services to corporations and non-profit organizations.

Dan Carpenter is a columnist for the *Indianapolis Star,* an Indianapolis native, and a graduate of Cathedral High School and Marquette University. He is the author of *Hard Pieces: Dan Carpenter's Indiana* and a contributor to *Falling toward Grace,* both from Indiana University Press. He lives in Indianapolis with his wife, Mary, and children, Patrick and Erin.

Judith Vale Newton is author of *The Hoosier Group: Five American Painters* and editor of *You Be the Judge.* She is co-author of *Beyond Realism: The Life and Art of Frederik Grue* and *A Grand Tradition: The Art and Artists of the Hoosier Salon, 1925–1990.* Former editor-in-chief of *Arts Indiana* and a columnist for *The Saturday Evening Post,* Newton has contributed to such publications as *ARTnews, Antique Review, Traces of Indiana,* and *Midwestern History.*

Contributing Writers

Barbara Shoup is the author of four novels: *Night Watch, Wish You Were Here, Stranded in Harmony,* and *Faithful Women.* She has been the writer-in-residence at Broad Ripple High School Center for the Humanities since 1982.

Lawrence S. Connor is a lifelong Indianapolis resident. He spent forty-one years at the *Indianapolis Star,* the last eleven as managing editor, before retiring in 1990. He writes occasional book reviews for the paper and is the author of *Hampton Court: Growing Up Catholic in Indianapolis between the Wars.*

Alissa Cook was born and raised in Indianapolis. She currently is a student at Ball State University in Muncie, Indiana.

Khemli Ezell was an English major at Indiana University–Purdue University Indianapolis in the graduating class of 2001.

Kim Charles Ferrill is a fine-art photographer who has illustrated several books, been exhibited in museums and galleries, and is author of the forthcoming book, *Sacred Heartland: A Photographer's Journey.* His work has been featured on PBS and in *The New Yorker Magazine,* and is in numerous institutional and private collections.

Rita Kohn is a writer with fourteen published books and two dozen produced plays. She is a senior writer with *NUVO Newsweekly* in Indianapolis. Kohn currently is editor of *Ohio River Books.*

Priscilla Lindsay is the associate artistic director at the Indiana Repertory Theatre, where she acts, directs, and leads many of the education programs. She has been a resident artist at the IRT for twenty-four years, in which time she has acted in more than forty-five plays.

Cheryl Soden Moreland is a member of the Writers' Center of Indiana. She has written essays for the *Indianapolis Star* and has published poetry. She works for the Indianapolis–Marion County Public Library.

Agate Nesaule was born in Latvia, went with her parents to Germany during the final year of World War II, and spent the next five years in Displaced Persons camps. She came to the United States and Indianapolis in 1950, when she was twelve. Educated at Indiana University and the University of Wisconsin–Madison, she was a Professor of English and of Women's Studies at the University of Wisconsin–Whitewater. Her memoir, *A Woman in Amber: Healing the Trauma of War and Exile,* won a 1996 American Book Award.

Tam Lin Neville taught for six years as a Creative Writing Teaching Fellow at Butler University and was awarded a Master Artist Fellowship by the Indiana Arts Commission. Her poems and essays have been published in many national journals. Her book of poems, *Journey Cake,* was published in 1998.

Aaren Yeatts Perry was born and raised in Indianapolis, where he attended Shortridge High School. He is a poet, writer, cultural activist, and freelance teacher of poetry and writing to all ages at schools and colleges. He is the author of *Poetry across the Curriculum: An Action Guide for Elementary Teachers.*

Nelson Price is the author of *Indiana Legends: Famous Hoosiers from Johnny Appleseed to David Letterman* and *Indianapolis: Leading the Way.* He is also a feature writer for the *Indianapolis Star.* Nelson has won more than forty state, local, civic, and national awards for his profiles of newsmakers.

Fran Quigley is a lifelong resident of Indianapolis. He has served as an anti-poverty lawyer in both the criminal and civil courts. Currently, he is an associate editor at *NUVO Newsweekly.*

S. K. Robisch is an assistant professor of American Literature and Ecological Literature at Purdue University, and has taught as a visiting professor at Butler University. He has published both fiction and criticism.

Ebony Utley was born and raised in Indianapolis. She is a graduate of Broad Ripple High School Center for the Humanities and the Performing Arts, and currently is a Wells Scholar at Indiana University.

Kate Webb has lived in Indianapolis since 1972. She presently is vice president of development at Laverna Lodge, an extended care residential treatment facility for chemically dependent men in greater Indianapolis.

Elizabeth Weber's most recent essay appeared in the anthology *The Human Tradition in the Vietnam Era.* She is the author of a book of poems, *Small Mercies.* She teaches creative writing at the University of Indianapolis, where she is an associate professor of English and co-directs the Kellogg Writers Series.

Greg Weber is a thirteen-year veteran of the Indianapolis Police Department. In addition, he is an active member of the Writers' Center of Indiana, where he concentrates his writing efforts on poetry.

Kate Shoup Welsh, born and raised in Indianapolis, is a freelance writer and editor. During the course of her career, she has penned three computer books and was the sports editor for *Nuvo Newsweekly.*

Additional Contributors

Hande Birkalan graduated from Bosphorus University with a B.A. in Turkish Language and Literature. She earned her Ph.D. at the Indiana University Folklore Institute in 1999. She currently is an assistant professor at the Yeditepe University Department of English in Istanbul, Turkey. She has two forthcoming books: *Homemaking and Story Telling in a Gecekondu* and *Pertev Naili Boratav and His Contributions to Turkish Folklore.*

Sharon Mishkin was born in Queens, New York, and grew up in Brooklyn. She graduated from Cornell University and received M.S. and Ph.D. degrees from Indiana University. She and her husband moved in Indianapolis in 1964. Their three children grew up in Indianapolis.